T0322071

COOKING
WITH
Nonna

GIUSEPPE FEDERICI

FOR MY (AND EVERY) NONNA

COOKING
WITH
Nonna

CLASSIC ITALIAN RECIPES
WITH A **PLANT-BASED** TWIST

GIUSEPPE FEDERICI

PHOTOGRAPHY BY DAVID LOFTUS

MICHAEL JOSEPH

CONTENTS

BENVENUTO

Welcome to *Cooking with Nonna*! Maybe someone gifted it to you or you're a fan of my videos on social media, or maybe you just thought who's that handsome fella on the front cover? However this book has ended up in your hands – thank you for picking it up! Making it has been a real adventure, including many hours spent in the kitchen and many more sat at my laptop and at photoshoots in London and Sicily (tough job, eh?). Now that it's out there, I'm so proud of the result and I can't wait to hear what you think.

The recipes you'll find within these pages are special. Authentic Italian recipes passed down and honed from generation to generation, but slightly adapted for a plant-based diet. It's the kind of food that I worried I would never get to eat again when I switched to a plant-based diet, so even if no one buys it (please buy it!), at least I've got them all written down in a handy package for future use!

Writing my first cookbook was always going to be a big deal, but the fact that I've done it with my nonna (grandma), Marianna, makes it something that I will treasure forever. Whether cooking in her restaurant or for the family sat round her crowded kitchen table every Sunday, Nonna has always made food that brings people together. So the fact that these recipes will now be doing this in kitchens all over the world is something that brings me great pride and it is a real testament to her legacy.

It's been massively rewarding, but it hasn't always been the easiest of processes. Nonna, like many cooks of her generation, is an instinctive cook. A pinch of this, a handful of that, always resulting in delicious dishes. A wonderful skill in a home cook, slightly problematic when you want to write a cookbook! So a big part of the challenge has been to standardize the recipes, make sure they taste great time after time and get them down on paper in a way that's easy to follow.

This book is a real collaboration. Many of the recipes are based on Nonna originals (labelled with a small `Approved by Nonna´ stamp in the corner of the page), but lots of others are recipes that I've developed from scratch, taking inspiration from Italian cuisine and my love of plant-based dishes.

Nonna wouldn't necessarily know how to make a plant-based cannoli (see page 232), for example, but she's tasted it all and given it her stamp of approval – meaning she said 'very nice!' or 'lov-er-ly!' when she tried it.

I've tried to stick to all-natural ingredients and authentic methods, though if you want a shortcut and would rather use ready-made plant-based mince or meatballs then that's fine too. Where possible, I've given you both options.

Most importantly, this book is for everyone. Whether you're fully plant-based, trying to do it a few times a week or just have some plant-based guests coming round for dinner and need some inspiration, you'll find a world of delicious, authentic Italian food in these pages. I hope you enjoy *Cooking with Nonna* as much as I do.

Buon appetito!

Sepps x

BEFORE NONNA WAS NONNA...

. . . she was Marianna Pletto, born on 7 February 1939 in a very small, very busy house in the town of Favara, in the province of Agrigento in southern Sicily. The first of six children, Marianna spent her early years watching her mother and her own nonna cook in the kitchen of their tiny house, being taught to sew by the local nuns, helping her mother with chores and, eventually, looking after the siblings who arrived at fairly reliable four-year intervals for the next eighteen years. A brother, Francesco, came first, followed by four sisters: Felicina, Lillina, Isabella and Guiseppina.

Family meals in that little house were all cooked by Marianna's mother and nonna, and the table would be filled with heaped bowls of delicious pasta, hearty soups rich in veg and pulses, and freshly baked bread. Twice a week, Marianna would accompany her mother to the communal town bread oven, a place where the women of the town would gather to bake fresh loaves and miscati rolls (see page 95), catch up with friends, and exchange stories, recipes and town gossip. The produce that was cooked and served at that family table changed with the seasons, the hot summer months bringing an abundance of fragrant tomatoes, courgettes and aubergines, while autumn and winter gave way to mushrooms, fennel, root vegetables and pulses. It was here that Marianna learned to cook, first watching and then helping her mother as the number of hungry mouths around the table grew.

Marianna was raised Catholic, and religious festivals and celebrations were a social high point for the entire community in Favara. One festival, the Festa di San Giuseppe (guess who I'm named after?!), is a time of great celebration and is held to give thanks to San Giuseppe (Saint Joseph), a Catholic saint who, story has it, responded to the prayers of countless hungry Sicilians at a time of drought and brought on rain, thus bringing back the crops and ending the famine. In celebration of the day, a great feast is held, with Minestra di San Giuseppe (see page 88) and Sfinci di San Giuseppe (see page 216) among the delicacies served.

It was at the Feast of San Giuseppe where Marianna first met a strapping young man by the name of Antonio Sgarito – a man who I now know as Nonno. He was returning to his hometown of Favara from the UK, where he had travelled two years earlier to find work in the mines. Unbeknownst to Marianna, he had more

on his agenda than simply catching up with family and friends, as his sister had told him about a very pretty girl in the town who she thought he should meet. That girl was, of course, Marianna, but times being different, Antonio could not approach her directly, so instead he went to her father and requested his permission to woo his daughter. A request that Marianna's father, thankfully, granted.

Marianna and Antonio got engaged on the day they met (wild, I know!), but after just a few days of courtship their affair was hastily put on hold as Antonio returned to England to work again in the mines and save for his impending nuptials. The young couple sent love letters several times a week, getting to know each other and making plans for their life together, each letter bringing a few rays of warm Sicilian sun to Antonio in chilly Staffordshire. With every letter, Marianna and Antonio's love for each other grew, and a year later Antonio returned to Favara and the couple were married. A whistlestop honeymoon in Palermo later and Marianna found herself leaving Sicily for the first time, aged just eighteen, and travelling to her new home in England to start her exciting new life as Marianna Sgarito.

She HATED it! It was October 1957, and Stoke-on-Trent was cold, wet, dark and windy – a far cry from the warm coastal climate that Nonna was used to. Though it's hard to imagine now, Italian cuisine was largely unknown in 1950s Britain and the shops near Marianna's new home didn't carry the ingredients she needed to recreate her beloved family recipes. Salvation came in the shape of an Italian man with a van. A van loaded with olive oil, cheese and pasta, and all of the things that Marianna was so desperately craving. That van was a lifeline to the Italian community who had been drawn to the UK to work in the mines. Work in Sicily was scarce at the time and the community was grateful for the opportunity to work and earn money, but for many, Marianna and Antonio included, that van provided the taste of home that they so needed.

A year after they first started their married life in the UK, Antonio decided it was time to leave the mines and start working for himself. He and Marianna loved food, but the classic Italian food they loved was unfamiliar to UK customers, so they opted instead for a safer bet: fish and chips! Their first venture, a mobile fish and chip van, was a success, and they soon expanded into a permanent site called Roman Barbecue. It was here that they first tried to sell their beloved Italian food, which, to their disappointment, proved to be unpopular with the locals. Instead, they installed a huge rotisserie oven from which they sold roast chicken and chips.

Roman Barbecue was eventually sold in 1972, and Nonno set up his own ice cream factory selling ice cream, lollies, and cones to the local ice cream men. Dad's dad (who was a local ice cream man) was one of his regular customers. The factory was very successful for about five years, until a hot summer in 1977 melted all the stock. Shortly after that he decided to sell up, by which time Marianna and Antonio's own family had grown to include six children of their own, my mother, Norina, among them. The next few years were dedicated to raising those children, Antonio still driving the original fish and chip van to pay the bills. Because the fish and chip van was doing so well, they eventually expanded and bought a permanent location, which was very successful for many years.

By the early 1980s the world had begun to open up and people had started to travel abroad more widely. Sensing this growing appetite for travel and interest in Italian cuisine, Marianna and Antonio decided in 1982 that now was the time to share their food with the world, converting the chip shop into La Favorita, the classic Italian taverna that they had always dreamed of.

La Favorita was an immediate hit, fully booked every weekend by people wanting to feast on authentic lasagne, carbonara and tiramisu. It had an open kitchen and customers could watch Marianna working her magic night after night while Antonio ruled the front of house, chatting with the regulars and charming newcomers with complimentary shots of limoncello and flaming sambuca to end their night. The restaurant was a typical Italian: red-checked tablecloths, sputtering candles housed in straw-bound bottles of Chianti and the Italian flag proudly displayed on the windows.

The restaurant was a haven for Marianna and Antonio, their own little Italy in Stoke-on-Trent. The days were long, often lasting into the early hours of the morning, but it was a real family business with everyone pulling together to help out where they could. Life went on this way for a long time. Marianna and Antonio's children eventually started having children of their own, but through it all La Favorita remained at the centre of family life, the site of family birthday parties, christenings and other celebrations. My own sister's birthday was celebrated there in 1996, just one year before I was born. But though Marianna (now officially a nonna!) loved the restaurant, she was tired and wanted to slow down. By then all of their children had found their own ways in life and none of them could be convinced to take on the restaurant, so the decision was made to sell it in 1996. A year later I was born.

AND THEN THERE WAS SEPPS...

. . . short for Giuseppe (my family calls me Joe, but you can't – sorry!). I arrived on the scene in 1997, just a year after La Favorita had been sold on. It's a shame that I never got to visit the restaurant, but I grew up eating the same food, cooked by the same woman, so I guess that I got a pretty good deal! This is jumping ahead, but I think the spirit of the restaurant still lives on in Nonna's kitchen and my own, and I'd love nothing more than to open my own plant-based outpost of La Favorita some day. If I do, please come visit!

For as long as I can remember, food has always been at the centre of our family life, especially where Nonna is involved. The whole family, including my aunts, uncles and cousins, would gather at Nonna's every Sunday for lunch. Being British Italians, we feasted on the best of both worlds – it wasn't until relatively recently that I realized other families don't start their traditional Sunday roast with a plate of pasta or a hefty slab of lasagne!

When my elder sister Elisia and I were very young, Nonna and Nonno were our babysitters. My parents, Gari and Norina, both worked full time, my dad running the family ice-cream business (more on that later) and my mum working in retail, so our weekends and after-school hours were often spent at Nonna's. I've always loved my food, and at Nonna's I could eat to my heart's content. Every meal was cooked from scratch with love; there was always some kind of pasta, usually pasta al sugo (page 124) but often pasta con i broccoli (page 166), pasta con lenticchie (page 157), lasagne (page 150) or cannelloni (page 170), as well as fresh bread, minestra and a whole cupboard full of biscuits if I found any room between meals. (It's honestly a good job that I got into exercise!) We were always sampling the food as she cooked or licking the beaters when she made tiramisu (page 223), so we made sure never to be far from the kitchen. Her English isn't brilliant and our Italian is patchy, but we muddled through, our mutual love of Nonna's delicious food bridging any gaps in communication.

During the summer holidays, my sister and I would help our dad out in the ice-cream factory or working in one of the vans, serving ice cream or doughnuts in the local town centre. One of my earliest memories is of my dad letting us 'sample' the ice cream to make sure it got the official Federici stamp of approval before it went on sale. It always did!

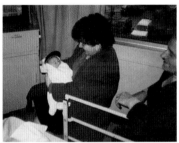

WHY PLANT-BASED?

We've always been a health-conscious family, so when my dad was diagnosed with colon cancer in 2014, it came as a huge shock and we all rallied round to try and help in any way we could. He began treatment immediately, but I wanted to see if there was anything else we could be doing as a family to help. After doing lots of research, I learned that foods like processed meat (salami, bacon and ham) and red meat (beef) were classified as class-1 and class-2 carcinogens by the World Health Organization. I also learned that eating a wholefood, plant-based diet could significantly reduce your risk of colon cancer and other diseases like heart disease. After watching a few documentaries about the meat and dairy industries, I was feeling less than great about my diet as a result, so I suggested to my family that we give plant-based eating a try. It didn't happen overnight, but soon I was eating a fully plant-based diet and my family started to follow suit. Within a year, my dad was in remission – there are many factors that contributed to this and it's likely he was very lucky, but I do believe that the switch to plant-based eating played a part. And, even without his illness, we all feel happier and healthier eating this way.

Now, the above makes it sound like the process of making the switch to plant-based eating was easy. It really wasn't, but it was a necessity. As a family we were used to eating traditional Italian dishes, rich in meat and dairy, every day of the week. Those dishes were part of our DNA, so cutting them out simply wasn't an option. I needed to find a way to still eat the food that I had grown up eating, and I knew that there was only one person who could help me: Nonna!

The wonderful thing about Italian food is that, though you might not guess it, a lot is naturally vegan anyway. Traditionally this is seasonal peasant food, otherwise known as *cucina povera* – meat and dairy are expensive, so the heart of many Italian dishes is already vegetarian or vegan. Rich tomato sauces, silky aubergines, hearty soups with pulses and legumes, all drizzled with extra virgin olive oil. Pasta without eggs is easy, and plant-based cheese has never been better. You just need a bit of expertise, and I have someone with eighty-five years' experience!

I started my page as a way to show people what I ate on a plant-based diet. My intention was never to put Nonna on my social channels, simply to note down her recipes, but one day I was filming her cooking in the kitchen and I decided to post it on a whim. It was an immediate hit. In fact, honestly, it was a bit overwhelming! People responded instantly to the clear joy that sharing this food gave her, how warm and natural she is on camera. My following started to grow and soon there were millions of people watching us cook our family's food week after week. And we're only just starting our journey!

It has been the greatest privilege to work with Nonna in this way. We've always been close, but this has brought us even closer together and it has opened the door to so many amazing opportunities: cooking live on TV, having Nonna on stage with me to win Fortnum & Mason's Creator of the Year Award, meeting the King and Queen (!!!) and, now, writing this book. The greatest gift, though, is sharing with the world just how special Nonna is, something that my family have known for a long time.

MEET THE FAMILY

So, you've met me and Nonna but we're not the only ones who have contributed recipes to this book. Pulling this collection of dishes together has been a real family affair, and just as Nonna is the matriarch of our family, her sisters (my great-aunts) are the heads of their respective branches. Put these five women in a room and ask them the best way to boil pasta and you'll get a sore ear and five very different answers, but each of them so skilled and knowledgeable about Italian food that I had to ask them each to contribute a recipe to the book. Find out more about each of them on the next page.

FELICINA

The next oldest sister after Nonna, Aunt Felicina is warm, bubbly and a wonderful hostess who always makes sure every guest has a glass in their hand and a plate of something delicious in front of them. Living in Favara, Felicina moved to England for six months to help when Nonna and Nonno opened their first restaurant, Roman Barbecue.

Favourite dish: Minestra di San Giuseppe (see page 88)

LILLINA

Next in line is Lillina. Lillina is a schoolteacher by trade and is very caring of her family, always on the phone to check that everyone is OK. Being the third sister, and some fourteen years younger than Nonna, she is a little quieter than her elder siblings, but more out of necessity than anything else!

Favourite dish: Cobaita (see page 266)

ISABELLA

Isabella was only four years old when Nonna left Sicily and moved to England, but they grew very close when Isabella moved to the UK to pursue a career in teaching. She stayed in England for twenty years but eventually moved back to Sicily. Of all my great-aunts she speaks the best English so is a wonderful asset in keeping conversation going when everyone gets together.

Favourite dish: Patate al forno (see page 204)

GIUSEPPINA

Nonna's youngest sister, Giuseppina, was born after Nonna had moved to the UK and is, in fact, one month younger than Nonna's own eldest child, Carmelina. The family resemblance is so strong that many thought the two babies were twins, though technically the younger baby was the older one's aunt!

Favourite dish: Miscati (see page 95)

ZIA FELICINA

ZIA LILLINA

ZIA ISABELLA

ZIA GIUSEPPINA

THE PLANT-BASED ITALIAN PANTRY

The great thing about the recipes in this book is that you'll probably already have a lot of the things you need in your kitchen cupboards or fridge. There are a few fancier items that I suggest, some of the vegan cheeses for example, but nothing that shouldn't be readily available in your local shop. I've listed below a few things Nonna and I always try to have on hand. If you've got a few of these ready to go, then you should be able to make most of the recipes in this book without any extra trips to the shops!

Cupboard Ingredients

TINNED CHOPPED TOMATOES

Quite possibly the most important ingredient in this book. Nonna has used at least two tins every day for the last sixty-five years, which is about 50,000. That's a lot of tomatoes! You can buy them in multipacks to save on cost and they last for ages. You can buy posh ones, but Nonna just uses own-brand, so I'd recommend trying out different brands until you find your favourite.

EXTRA VIRGIN OLIVE OIL

The taste of Italy in a bottle. If you can, I'd recommend spending a bit more money to get the good stuff. It's perfect for salads, drizzling over dishes at the end or using sparingly to roast vegetables in the oven.

VEGETABLE OIL

Cheaper than olive oil and with less flavour, this is perfect for any frying (deep or shallow) where you don't need the dominant flavours of olive oil. Nonna mostly uses this for frying thirsty aubergines.

LENTILS AND BEANS (DRIED AND TINNED)

Dried beans and legumes are cheaper and last way longer than the tinned ones. Tinned are great for when you're in a rush as they don't need soaking and are ready to eat right away. Both types can sit in your cupboard for ages, waiting to bring heft and flavour to any dish. They are a great source of plant-based protein and are perfect in hearty winter dishes, or any soup or stew.

DRIED PASTA

All the shapes. Most dried pasta is vegan-friendly – just check the ingredients to make sure before putting it in your basket. For most of the recipes in this book, the pasta shapes are fairly interchangeable, though some, like a lasagne or a cannelloni, do need a specific shape. As a general rule, Nonna always keeps penne, farfalle, spaghetti, linguine, lasagne sheets and cannelloni tubes in stock. You'll notice in some recipes that I've listed a number alongside the type of pasta; this is because certain pasta shapes have different sizes or grades. I've given these as an ideal if you're going to the shops and buying the pasta new, but always use what you have on hand at home first.

ARBORIO RICE

Short, plump arborio is the perfect grain for any risotto (page 188) or the base of arancini (page 72). Briefly toasted and then cooked slowly, adding a ladleful of stock at a time, the resulting rice will be creamy, flavourful and with the perfect amount of bite. **Fun fact:** I used to think arborio rice was actually called *absorbio* rice because of how much liquid it absorbs!

DRIED HERBS AND SPICES

My pantry always has a stock of the following: dried parsley, basil, bay leaves, oregano and fennel seeds. Fresh herbs are wonderful, but they can be expensive and don't last long. Nonna also keeps fresh basil and parsley in a ziplock bag in the freezer, which can be used anytime you require dried or fresh herbs.

DRIED BREADCRUMBS

You can buy dried Italian breadcrumbs, otherwise known as fine Italian breadcrumbs or *pangrattato,* though Nonna grates her own stale bread and keeps it in a dry tin with a bay leaf to absorb the moisture. Breadcrumbs are wonderful for breading vegetables or tofu before frying or for creating a crunchy *pangrattato* to top pasta dishes.

FLOUR

Plain flour, extra-strong bread flour and Tipo 00 extra-fine flour. I generally have all three of these in the cupboard. Plain flour is for everyday cooking and great for everything from baking biscuits to breading vegetables and thickening sauces. Bread flour (unsurprisingly!) is great for bread. It forms strong gluten bonds and makes for robust, springy dough. Tipo 00 flour is wonderful for delicate homemade pasta dough (page 118), as it is milled superfine so leaves you with a silky-smooth texture.

VINEGAR

Red wine vinegar, white wine vinegar, balsamic vinegar and balsamic glaze. All are wonderful for dressing salads, drizzling over pasta or adding a hit of acid to cut through the richness of a sauce.

VEGETABLE STOCK CUBES

Yes, in an ideal world you'd make your own, but sometimes it's Tuesday night and you just want to get dinner on the table. Nonna uses the small square cubes and often crumbles them into a bubbling dish, but you can also use veg stock powder, which works just as well!

SALT

As a general rule, fine salt for cooking and seasoning pasta water (it should be as salty as the sea). Flaky sea salt for serving. Whatever you use, make sure you season your food!

COFFEE (FOR DRINKING NOT COOKING)

Ground or beans, depending on your home set-up. Don't tell anyone (especially anyone Italian), but Nonna and I prefer decaffeinated coffee, simply because we enjoy the taste and like to drink it often while also being able to sleep at night.

Fresh Ingredients

ONIONS

White, red, shallots, spring onions. Onions are the starting point of so many dishes and can add so much flavour to any dish. Nonna's go-to onion is an echalion shallot, as she prefers the subtle sweet flavour. One top Nonna tip is to never keep them in the fridge as it dulls their flavour.

GARLIC

A must in any Italian kitchen. Use copiously. As with onion, keeping it in the fridge can dull its flavour.

CARROTS

Carrots add a mellow, earthy sweetness to dishes, especially when cooked down slowly over time. Along with onion and celery, the base ingredients in a soffritto.

CELERY

Crisp and crunchy, celery adds a mild saltiness when cooked down into a sauce. Often added at the beginning of a dish along with onions and carrots.

POTATOES

Wonderful for making gnocchi (see page 142), for roasting as a side dish or to thicken a soup or stew. Nonna always keeps a large bag out of the fridge and adds an apple to prevent them from sprouting.

AUBERGINES

One of the most underrated vegetables. A staple ingredient in many classic Sicilian dishes, silky aubergines are wonderful to have on hand to make caponata (page 55), pasta alla Norma (page 130) or melanzane alla parmigiana (page 184). All the good stuff!

FENNEL

Fennel adds a subtle aniseed flavour and is wonderful roasted (see page 199) or even served raw as part of a salad (see page 47). The feathery tops can be chopped and used as a delicious garnish.

FRESH HERBS

Parsley, basil, bay leaves. The list could go on, but these three are the ones that I always have to hand. If you are lucky enough to have a garden or even a spare windowsill, you could have a go at growing your own. If you're buying from the supermarket, keeping any cut stems in water will prolong their life and keep them fresh for longer.

PLANT-BASED CHEESE

Vegan cheese used to be a bit naff and plastic-tasting, but that's changed! There are many wonderful plant-based cheeses on the market now and it's possible to find a vegan alternative for almost any variety. I particularly like the brand Julienne Bruno, which specializes in plant-based creations such as Burella and Crematta. Other good brands are Sheese and Smoked Applewood, which melts really well. If you're going to be using a lot of plant-based Parmesan or ricotta, then I would urge you to have a go at making your own using the recipes overleaf.

3. Transfer to an airtight container and store in the fridge until you're ready to sprinkle on your favourite pastas and salads, or, if you're like me, on slices of cucumber for a refreshing salty snack.

Cashew Ricotta

I grew up with ricotta being a really special treat which Nonna absolutely loves. It's a silky-soft and slightly sweet cheese that's used in many sweet and savoury dishes. Literally translating to `recooked', ricotta is a unique Italian cheese because it's traditionally made with the leftover curdled proteins from the production of other cheeses, so we use a similar technique to make the soy milk ricotta version. I prefer the texture of this but it does take a bit of effort, so we've also included a much easier version made with soaked cashews, which is just as tasty and super versatile!

MAKES: *6 servings*
PREP TIME: *4 hours or overnight*

INGREDIENTS ◆

180g raw cashews
1 tsp nutritional yeast
a pinch of garlic powder
salt to taste

1. Soak the cashew nuts in cold water overnight or in warm water for at least 4 hours.

Cashew Parmesan

This is a healthy homemade crumble that satisfies that salty craving and lasts for weeks in the fridge in an air-tight container.

MAKES: *10 servings*
PREP TIME: *5 mins*

INGREDIENTS ◆

150g raw cashews
3 tbsp nutritional yeast
1 tsp garlic powder
1½ tsp onion powder
1 tsp flaky sea salt

1. Place all the ingredients in a food processor or a high-speed blender.
2. Blend for around 30–60 seconds, until a fine powder is formed.

2. Drain the cashews, then place them in a food processor with 130ml cold water, nutritional yeast, garlic powder and salt, and pulse until creamy but still with some texture. Add a splash more water if you want a looser and creamier ricotta.

3. Season to taste.

Soy Ricotta

MAKES: *4 servings*
PREP TIME: *2 mins*
COOKING TIME: *35 mins + overnight resting*

INGREDIENTS ◆

1 litre unsweetened soy milk
1 tsp fine salt
3 tbsp apple cider vinegar

I. Give your bottle of soy milk a little shake, then pour it into a saucepan over a medium heat and bring to the boil. This should take about 10 minutes. Gently stir every few minutes with a wooden spoon so it doesn't stick to the bottom.

2. Once just boiling, remove from the heat and very gently stir in the salt and apple cider vinegar. You should start to see the soy milk separate and curds start to form. This should take about 30 seconds to a minute.

3. Set the pot aside for 15 minutes without stirring.

4. Line a large sieve with a piece of muslin cheesecloth or a clean tea towel. Pour the curdled soy milk into the cloth.

5. Set the sieve over a large bowl and leave for 10 minutes for the majority of the liquid to drain into the bowl. Discard the liquid that collects in the bowl.

6. Gather the corners of the cloth together and tie with string to form a bag. Suspend the bag over the bowl overnight in the fridge so the ricotta can continue to drain.

7. The next day your ricotta is ready to use in pasta, cannoli or cannelloni!

ANTIPASTI E INSALATE

Appetizers & Salads

Nonna
APPROVED

Anything *sott'olio* means submerged in oil – and it's a common method used across Italy to preserve vegetables. Nonna loves to make jars of this to serve in salads, with bread or on pasta.

CARCIOFI SOTT'OLIO
Artichokes in Oil

MAKES: *1 large jar*
PREP TIME: *15 mins*
COOKING TIME: *20 mins*

INGREDIENTS ◆

1 lemon
400g ripe artichokes
3 small radishes
1 stalk of celery
1 small carrot
250ml white vinegar
salt and black pepper
1 tsp dried oregano
2 cloves of garlic, crushed
extra virgin olive oil

1. Add the juice of ½ a lemon to a large bowl of cold water. This will help prevent the artichoke bits from going brown.

2. Slice the thick green stems off the artichokes, then carefully peel off the tougher outer petals by tearing them away from the middle. You should be left with a teardrop-shaped artichoke with petals that are much lighter in colour.

3. Slice off the tip of the artichoke about 3cm up from the base of the stem, then carefully cut out the fluffy bits left in the centre. You want to get rid of as much of these fluffy bits as possible!

4. Cut the artichoke into quarters, and add them to the bowl of lemon water. Repeat with the rest of the artichokes.

5. Wash the veg and peel the carrot. Slice the radishes and carrot into thin discs. Slice the celery in half lengthways, then cut into batons about 3cm long. Put the prepared veg aside.

6. Add the white vinegar to a pan with 500ml of water and the juice of the remaining ½ a lemon.

7. Drain the artichokes and add them to the pan along with 1 tablespoon of salt. Bring to the boil, then simmer for 10 minutes. Drain the artichokes again once they begin to turn lighter in colour, and transfer them to a large bowl.

8. Add the prepared radish, celery, carrot and crushed garlic to the bowl with 1 teaspoon of salt, a pinch of black pepper and 1 teaspoon of dried oregano.

9. Add a drizzle of olive oil to the bowl and mix everything together. Now, transfer all the veg to a jar, fill it with oil to cover and close the lid so it's airtight. Store in the fridge and it will last for months!

Nduja (pronounced en-doo-ya) is an Italian sausage similar to chorizo that originates from Calabria. It's soft in texture and spreadable. This plant-based version is made from a few simple ingredients that all bring their own rich flavours and textures to create this delicious alternative, plus it uses tempeh so it's super-high in protein too! You can serve this with crusty bread, on top of pizza or even as a pasta sauce just loosened with some pasta water and cream.

NDUJA
Homemade Vegan Nduja

SERVES: *4*
PREP TIME: *15 mins*

INGREDIENTS ◆

1 vegetable stock cube

salt and black pepper

100g tempeh

168g sun-dried tomatoes (208g jar, drained weight), plus 1 tbsp of the oil

1 jarred roasted red pepper

75g pitted Kalamata olives

2 tsp rose harissa paste

1 tbsp extra virgin olive oil

1 tsp chilli flakes

1 tsp smoked paprika

½ tsp cayenne pepper

juice of ½ a lemon

40g breadcrumbs

1. Bring a pan of water to the boil, and add the veg stock cube and a pinch of salt. Add the tempeh to the pan and simmer gently for 10 minutes (it won't change appearance, it will just go a little firmer, absorb the flavours and lose its bitter earthy taste).

2. While the tempeh is cooking, put all the remaining ingredients into a food processor.

3. Once the tempeh has simmered for 10 minutes, take it out, tap it dry with kitchen paper, then break it into a few chunks and add to the food processor.

4. Process everything on the pulse setting – you don't want it all to turn to mush, but you still want everything combined. Stop when the tempeh has broken down into small crumbs.

5. If serving with pasta, simply put the nduja into a frying pan with the cooked pasta of your choice, along with a generous amount of pasta water and optionally some vegan cream cheese (like Philadelphia) to make it nice and creamy.

6. Alternatively, store in an airtight jar in the fridge, and enjoy as a dip with bread.

Aubergine is such an underrated vegetable – when cooked correctly, it can have a slight meaty texture and it absorbs so much flavour. Serve these cotolette di melanzane with pasta, as a side to a salad or simply on their own as a snack!

COTOLETTE DI MELANZANE
Breadcrumbed Aubergine

SERVES: *2–4*
PREP TIME: *15 mins*
COOKING TIME: *10 mins*

INGREDIENTS ◆

3 tbsp finely ground flaxseed

2 medium aubergines

2 tbsp fine sea salt

200g panko breadcrumbs

75g plain flour

100ml olive oil

1 tbsp finely chopped fresh parsley, or ½ tbsp dried parsley

1 lemon

salt

TIP ◆

Make sure to stay with the aubergines at all times when frying, and to top up with oil every time the pan dries out.

1. In a wide, medium-sized bowl mix together the ground flaxseed and 135ml of cold water. Stir thoroughly and set aside while you prepare the aubergines.

2. Trim the top and bottom of each aubergine, then cut them into 1cm discs.

3. Place all the aubergine discs in a large mixing bowl and cover with cold water (at least 1½ litres).

4. Sprinkle over 2 tablespoons of sea salt and mix with a wooden spoon or your hands so that all the salt dissolves. Set aside for 5–10 minutes. This helps to remove the bitterness from the aubergines. Remove the aubergines from the water and pat dry on kitchen paper or a tea towel.

5. Put the breadcrumbs into a large flat bowl or plate and put the flour into another. Put the bowl of flaxseed mix alongside.

6. Take one slice of aubergine and dip it into the flour, rolling it around to make sure it is all coated. Shake gently to remove any excess. Then dip briefly into the flaxseed mix to coat, again shaking off any excess. Finally place it in the breadcrumbs, making sure it is all covered. Press down firmly to help the crumbs stick, then transfer the breadcrumbed aubergine to a baking tray or plate. Repeat with the rest of the slices.

7. Take a large frying pan and add 75ml of olive oil. When the oil is hot, add as many breadcrumbed discs as will fit, and fry on both sides for 2–3 minutes, until golden brown. Try to avoid turning them over until fully cooked, as they will become quite fragile.

8. Place on a plate or tray lined with kitchen paper to help drain excess oil, and repeat until all the aubergine slices are cooked, topping up with the rest of the oil if the pan starts to look dry.

9. Serve with a pinch of salt, a scattering of fresh or dried parsley and a squeeze of lemon.

Nonna
APPROVED

Salads don't get much simpler than this one – traditionally made with just tomatoes, bread and a tangy dressing, it's the perfect light lunch on a hot summer's day. Nonna and I like to add artichoke hearts for an extra bite, and I'd recommend buying the best cherry or salad tomatoes you can find, and a fresh sourdough or ciabatta from a bakery if you can.

PANZANELLA
Italian Tomato & Bread Salad

SERVES: *2*
PREP TIME: *10 mins*
COOKING TIME: *10 mins*

INGREDIENTS ◆

4 salad tomatoes (the best quality you can find)

150g cherry tomatoes

200g sourdough or ciabatta

60ml olive oil

1 x 240g tin of artichoke hearts

2 cloves of garlic

2 tbsp balsamic vinegar

1 tsp dried oregano

salt and black pepper

a handful of fresh basil leaves

1. Cut the salad tomatoes into bite-size chunks and halve the cherry tomatoes. Place them in a large mixing bowl. Tear the bread into bite-size cubes.

2. Preheat your oven to 160°C fan/180°C. Place the torn bread pieces on a baking sheet and drizzle with olive oil. Toss to coat, then toast in the oven for about 10 minutes, or until they are golden and crispy. Let them cool.

3. Chop the artichoke hearts into bite-size pieces and add them to the bowl of tomatoes.

4. Add the cooled toasted bread to the tomatoes and artichokes.

5. Grate the garlic into a small bowl, and add the remaining olive oil, balsamic vinegar, dried oregano, salt and pepper. Mix together, then pour this dressing over the salad.

6. Gently toss everything together so that the bread soaks up the flavours. Let it sit for about 10 minutes to allow the flavours to mix.

7. Just before serving, tear the basil leaves over the salad.

A simple side dish great for family BBQs, light dinners, etc. It can be made in advance and eaten hot or cold – it keeps for a few days in the fridge. Nonna's eldest daughter, my Zia Carmelina, makes the best version of this, so this is her recipe!

PATATE E FAGIOLINI
Potato & Green Bean Salad

SERVES: *4*
PREP TIME: *5 mins*
COOKING TIME: *15 mins*

INGREDIENTS ◆

750g baby potatoes
200g green beans
2–3 spring onions
a handful of fresh parsley
50ml extra virgin olive oil
salt and black pepper

1. Bring a pan of water to the boil with a pinch of salt.

2. Cut the baby potatoes in half and add them to the pan of boiling water. Cook for 8–10 minutes, until fork tender.

3. Trim the green beans and add them to the potatoes when there's 5 minutes' cooking time left.

4. Finely slice the spring onions and parsley and put them into a large bowl, along with the olive oil, salt and pepper.

5. Drain the cooked potatoes and beans, making sure to get rid of all the water in the pan, then add them to the bowl, combine everything together and serve.

TIP ◆
Press the spring onion into the oil with a fork before adding the potatoes, so that the oil absorbs the flavours.

Nonna APPROVED

Fennel doesn't get as much attention as it deserves – it's such a unique vegetable that tastes completely different raw compared to roasted, but I love it both ways. This is a great salad to accompany a lasagne, as it's light, refreshing and bursting with flavour. I also love to make it during the summer for a light lunch, with the addition of some butter beans or tofu for extra protein. I served this salad at my first-ever restaurant residency at Norma, and everyone couldn't get enough!

INSALATA DI FINOCCHI E ARANCE
Fennel & Orange Salad

SERVES: 2
PREP TIME: 10 mins

INGREDIENTS ◆

1 large bulb of fennel

3 Sicilian oranges (or just the best quality oranges you can find)

½ a red onion

1 pack of rocket (60g)

Dressing
100ml freshly squeezed orange juice

2 tbsp red wine vinegar

2 tbsp agave syrup

1 tbsp Dijon mustard

a pinch of salt

1. Remove the outer layer of the fennel and slice off the base. Using a mandolin, if you have one, finely slice the fennel into a large mixing bowl. If you don't have one, just slice it as finely as you can, using a sharp knife, but be careful, please.

2. Slice the top and bottom off each orange, then, using a small sharp knife, carefully peel off the skin and cut off and discard any excess pith (the white stuff). Then slice the peel into small slivers. Add to the bowl along with the orange segments.

3. Finely slice the red onion and add to the bowl.

4. To make the dressing, put the orange juice, red wine vinegar, agave, mustard and salt into a jar, and give it a good shake to emulsify.

5. Just before serving, add the rocket to the bowl (last minute, to prevent it wilting), mix everything together, and drizzle with a generous amount of the dressing.

This refreshing yet comforting salad is made with one of my favourite salad leaves, radicchio. It's bursting with different flavours and textures and would work great before a plate of pasta! I developed this recipe with Giovann Attard, head chef at one of my favourite Italian restaurants in London, Norma – where I did my first ever restaurant pop-up.

INSALATA DI ZUCCA DELICA ARROSTO
Roasted Delica Pumpkin Salad

SERVES: *4*
PREP TIME: *10 mins*
COOKING TIME: *20 mins*

INGREDIENTS ◆

400–500g Delica pumpkin (or butternut squash)

olive oil

sea salt and black pepper

1 small red chilli

200g mixed radicchio leaves (red and white)

4 figs

50g roasted hazelnuts

seeds from 1 small pomegranate (or 80g pack)

Pomegranate dressing

50ml moscatel vinegar (or sherry vinegar)

50ml water

¼ tsp salt

40g caster sugar

50g extra virgin olive oil

100ml pomegranate molasses or balsamic glaze

1. Preheat the oven to 180°C fan/200°C.

2. Slice the pumpkin in half and scoop out the seeds. Cut the pumpkin into 2–4cm crescents.

3. Place on a lined baking tray, add a drizzle of olive oil and season with salt and black pepper. Combine everything together with your hands, then roast for 20 minutes, or until fork tender, flipping halfway.

4. Meanwhile, make the dressing: put the vinegar, water, salt and sugar into a bowl, then slowly pour in the oil while whisking until it emulsifies. Finally add the pomegranate molasses, and gently mix with a spoon.

5. Wash and dry the radicchio leaves. Quarter the figs and roughly chop the roasted hazelnuts. Put the radicchio into a large bowl and scatter over the figs, hazelnuts, pomegranate seeds and pumpkin slices.

6. Drizzle the salad with the pomegranate dressing, season with salt and pepper, and enjoy.

PRIMI PIATTI E CONTORNI

First Courses & Side Dishes

Involtini di melanzane sounds like some sort of Harry Potter spell, but it's actually a delicious dish that can be used as an antipasti. Nonna traditionally makes involtini with ham and cheese, so if you're looking to keep this old school you can simply use plant-based alternatives,. However, if you're looking for something impressive, try this walnut and sundried tomato filling that's packed with flavour.

INVOLTINI DI MELANZANE
Stuffed Aubergine Rolls

MAKES: *10–12*
PREP TIME: *20 mins*
COOKING TIME: *20 mins*

INGREDIENTS ◆

2 large aubergines

vegetable oil, for frying

sea salt

1 batch Nonna's pasta sauce (page 124)

a handful of grated vegan mozzarella (optional)

fresh basil leaves, to serve

cashew Parmesan (page 28) or grated vegan Parmesan, to serve

Walnut filling

100g chopped walnuts

80g sun-dried tomatoes

60g jarred roasted red pepper in oil (approx. 1 pepper)

3 tbsp extra virgin olive oil

2 tbsp plant-based cream cheese

½ tsp chilli flakes

1. Place the walnuts for the filling in a bowl and cover with cold water. Leave to soak for 1–3 hours.

2. To make the walnut filling, drain the walnuts and transfer to a food processor along with the rest of the filling ingredients. Pulse until well combined but still retaining some texture.

3. Cut the aubergines into long, 1cm-thick slices lengthways, about 6–8 slices per aubergine.

4. Coat the base of a non-stick griddle pan with vegetable oil and place over a medium heat. Once hot, fry the aubergine slices in batches for 1–2 minutes on each side, until golden, seasoning each slice with a pinch of salt. Transfer to a plate lined with kitchen paper to soak up any excess oil.

5. Transfer your batch of Nonna's pasta sauce to the base of a baking dish.

6. Add 2–3 teaspoons of the walnut filling to the bottom of each aubergine slice, then carefully roll up from the bottom and transfer to the baking dish, seam-side down to ensure that they do not unroll in the oven. Repeat until all of the aubergine slices have been used up, then sprinkle over the grated mozzarella, if using.

7. Bake at 180°C fan/200°C for 10–12 minutes, just long enough for the cheese to melt and the aubergines to get a little softer.

8. Top with fresh basil and grated vegan Parmesan, and enjoy.

Caponata is one of those dishes Nonna would always have somewhere in the house, stored in a glass jar. Think of it like bruschetta's cooler but less popular cousin – it's a soft, flavourful mix of vegetables that melts in your mouth, traditionally served with bread, though I can genuinely eat it with a spoon. It keeps for ages in an airtight container at the back of the fridge.

NONNA'S CAPONATA

Sicilian Caponata

SERVES: *4*
PREP TIME: *20 mins*
COOKING TIME: *20 mins*

INGREDIENTS ◆

3 large aubergines (approx. 800g)

2 stalks of celery, chopped (approx. 200g)

1 medium red onion or 2 banana shallots, finely sliced

1 red bell pepper

olive oil

3 tbsp red wine vinegar

½ tsp chilli flakes

sea salt and black pepper

1 x 400g tin of crushed tomatoes

300ml tomato passata

50g capers

100g pitted green olives

100g raisins or sultanas

1 tbsp sugar or agave syrup

15g parsley, finely chopped

1. Start by cutting the aubergines into 2–3cm cubes. Place them in a large bowl, generously and evenly coat with salt (about 1 tablespoon), and set aside.

2. Now prepare the rest of the vegetables: dice the celery (I like to slice each stalk down the middle first, then cut into 1–2cm pieces), onion (try not to cry) and red pepper.

3. Once the salted aubergines have been sitting for about 10 minutes, drain off any liquid that may have built up at the bottom of the bowl, and pat them dry. Heat some olive oil in a large frying pan on a medium heat and pan-fry them until nicely coloured and soft, which will take about 10 minutes – you want them soft but not mushy. You will probably need to work in batches. Transfer the aubergines to a large casserole dish and set aside.

4. Return the pan to the heat and add a tablespoon of olive oil. Add the celery to the pan and fry for 8–10 minutes, until softened, then transfer to the casserole dish.

5. Add the onions and peppers to the pan and fry for roughly 5 minutes, until the onions have softened and the peppers are softened and starting to char. Turn the heat to low and add the vinegar. Let it simmer for 1 minute, so the vinegar reduces and coats the onions. Transfer all the veg to the casserole dish and season with salt, pepper and a pinch of chilli flakes.

»

6. Add the tinned tomatoes and passata to the casserole dish, along with the capers, olives, raisins and sugar, and combine everything on a medium heat until just simmering. Lower the heat and cook for 20–30 minutes, until the vegetables are soft and the sauce is thick and glossy.

7. Once all the veg is very soft, add the parsley and mix again.

8. Leave to cool slightly, then enjoy with fresh bread, or store in an airtight container in the fridge.

TIPS ◆

Try adding a small square of dark chocolate when you add the tinned tomatoes, to give a creamy richness to the sauce.

Toasted pine nuts scattered over at the end add a nice crunch.

NONNA'S TOP TIP ◆

Boil the chunks of celery first to soften and help them cook more quickly.

Polpette are one of the few meat products I adored growing up – they're sort of like flat meatballs with extra flavour, made using breadcrumbs to make the meat go further. You can have these on their own but they also work brilliantly with our pesto alla Trapanese (page 141).

NONNA'S POLPETTE
Nonna's Meatballs

MAKES: *25–30*
PREP TIME: *15 mins*
COOKING TIME: *10 mins*

INGREDIENTS ◆

4 heaped tbsp ground flaxseed

15g vegan Parmesan

2 cloves of garlic

25g fresh parsley

350g vegan mince

130g fresh breadcrumbs

3 tbsp nutritional yeast (or more vegan Parmesan)

4 tbsp extra virgin olive oil

½ tbsp salt

½ tsp black pepper

25g plain wholemeal flour

4 tbsp plant-based milk

2 tbsp plain plant-based yoghurt

regular olive oil, for frying

1. Mix the ground flaxseed with 150ml of cold water and set aside for 5 minutes.

2. Meanwhile, finely grate the vegan Parmesan, grate the garlic and finely chop the parsley.

3. Put the vegan mince into a bowl with all the rest of the ingredients, apart from the oil for frying. With clean hands, combine until everything is mixed well together.

4. Shape into round balls a little smaller than a golf ball – if the mix is sticky, wet your hands a little to make it easier.

5. Cover the base of a medium frying pan with olive oil and bring to a medium-high heat. Fry the polpette in batches, flipping after 1–2 minutes, until they are all nicely coloured. It should look like a mini burger patty.

6. Serve with pesto alla Trapanese (page 141) or Nonna's pasta sauce (page 124).

Nonna
APPROVED

This dish is what my family and I call the emergency vegan order in Italian restaurants, as you can pretty much guarantee that any restaurant in Italy will have this on their menu and it's always cooked with just oil and garlic, so it's naturally vegan!

VERDURE GRIGLIATE
Mixed Grilled Veg

SERVES: *4*
PREP TIME: *10 mins*
COOKING TIME: *15 mins*

INGREDIENTS ◆

3 cloves of garlic, minced

30g fresh parsley, finely chopped

100ml extra virgin olive oil

1 tsp sea salt flakes

3 courgettes

2 aubergines

2 red peppers

1 yellow pepper

100g chestnut mushrooms, stems removed

1. Put the oil, garlic, salt and half the parsley into a large bowl and use a fork to mix everything together so that the garlic is well combined with the oil.

2. Place a griddle pan on a medium-high heat and leave it for a few minutes to heat up. Line a plate with a couple of sheets of kitchen paper.

3. Meanwhile, cut the top and base off the courgettes, then cut them into slices lengthways, approx. 3–4mm thick. (You can use a mandolin if you have one, but be very careful.) Brush the courgette slices with the oil mixture and place them on the hot griddle pan. Leave to fry for 2–3 minutes before checking – if you touch them before that, the grill lines won't look as good! Flip them over to cook on the other side. Repeat with the rest of the courgettes, placing them on the lined plate once they're done.

4. Give the pan a wipe clean if needed, then repeat the same process with the aubergines. I like to cut these into discs.

5. Repeat with the peppers and mushrooms, keeping the already cooked vegetables warm under the grill.

6. Place all the cooked veg on a large platter, then use any remaining oil mixture to lightly brush over the veg, and finish with a sprinkle of salt and the rest of the chopped parsley.

Bruschetta – pronounced broo-skett-ah – is one of those classic antipasti dishes that everyone loves, and was a popular starter at Nonna's restaurant. It's simple enough that pretty much anyone can make it, and it doesn't need any fancy ingredients. The perfect snack for those hot summer days when you want something quick and easy to nibble on. It's also ideal as a party snack, as you can prepare it ahead of time by making a large batch of topping and toasting the bread in bulk.

NONNA'S BRUSCHETTA

SERVES: *2–4*
PREP TIME: *15 mins*
COOKING TIME: *4–6 mins*

INGREDIENTS ◆

1 ciabatta loaf

150g vine-ripened cherry tomatoes

2 cloves of garlic

70g fresh basil

2 tbsp extra virgin olive oil, plus extra for drizzling

1. Preheat the oven to 160°C fan/180°C. While it's heating, cut your ciabatta in half lengthways. Then cut it into bite-size pieces diagonally, the perfect appetizer size.

2. Lay the pieces of ciabatta on a baking tray and bake in the oven until golden brown and crunchy. Approx. 4–6 minutes.

3. Quarter the cherry tomatoes and put them into a bowl. Grate in the garlic. Thinly slice the basil and add it to the bowl. Add the olive oil and mix everything together.

4. Remove the tray of ciabatta pieces from the oven and drizzle them with olive oil. Add your topping and enjoy.

TIP ◆

This is a pantry-friendly recipe, as you can use a variety of different toppings for your bruschetta, e.g. vegan cheese, olive paste and more. I also love to add plant-based cream cheese or burrata (my current favourite brand is Julienne Bruno).

Panelle are the ultimate Sicilian street food – made popular in the capital, Palermo, these light, fluffy and moreish fritters are naturally vegan. They're traditionally served in a bun with salt and lemon, but are equally delicious on their own. When we're in Sicily, Nonna and I often go for a walk in the evening to get some panelle, followed by gelato.

PANELLE
Crispy Chickpea Flour Fritters

MAKES: *about 24 pieces, each 8 x 5cm*
PREP TIME: *10 mins*
COOKING TIME: *20 mins*

INGREDIENTS ◆

200g chickpea flour (I use Doves Farm, which is available in supermarkets)

600ml cold water

½ tsp salt

freshly ground black pepper

2 tbsp fresh parsley, chopped

600ml vegetable oil

1 lemon, cut into wedges

1. First cut two sheets of greaseproof paper at least 55cm long and set aside.

2. Place the chickpea flour in a large mixing bowl. Make a well in the centre and gradually pour in the water while whisking all the time, until it has all been combined and you have a smooth, lump-free batter. Whisk in the salt and a generous amount of freshly ground black pepper.

3. Pour the batter into a medium saucepan and place over a medium heat. Whisk continuously until the batter is really thick and is starting to lift away from the sides and bottom of the pan when stirred. This should take around 10 minutes. Make sure to whisk vigorously once it begins to thicken, to make sure it stays smooth and the bottom of the pan doesn't burn.

4. Stir in the parsley, making sure it is well distributed.

5. Working very quickly, pour the hot chickpea batter into the middle of one of the sheets of greaseproof paper and place the other sheet on top. Using a rolling pin, rapidly roll the mixture between the sheets of paper until it is 5mm thick. It is important to work quickly because the batter will set rapidly as it cools.

6. Once it's completely cool, cut it lengthways into 8cm strips, then cut each strip into triangles. (Or rectangles if you prefer – both shapes are served in Sicily!)

7. Heat the vegetable oil in a large, heavy-based saucepan until it reaches 180°C. Carefully place 5 or 6 triangles of panelle in the oil and fry for 3–4 minutes, turning occasionally until they

»

are golden, crisp and have slightly puffed up. Remove with a slotted spoon and drain on kitchen paper.

8. Serve immediately, with a sprinkling of salt and a squeeze of lemon juice.

TIPS ◆

Use a big spatula to help you remove the chickpea batter slices from the baking paper, to prevent them from breaking, as they'll be very fragile at this point!

They also freeze very well – be sure to freeze them just after slicing, on a flat surface if possible, then they can be grouped/frozen in a container or ziplock freezer bag.

Made with just a few simple ingredients, zucchine fritte are a classic Italian street food that you can just keep on eating. They're best eaten as soon as they've begun to cool down after frying – so ideally make them when all your guests have arrived and you're ready to get cooking.

ZUCCHINE FRITTE
Courgette Fritters

SERVES: *3–4*
PREP TIME: *15 mins*
COOKING TIME: *10 mins*

INGREDIENTS ◆

3–4 medium courgettes

300g plain flour

1 tsp baking powder

1 tsp sea salt

a pinch of black pepper

350ml cold water

approx. 300ml vegetable/sunflower oil, for frying

juice of ½ a lemon

1. Cut off the ends of the courgettes, then carefully slice them lengthways approx. 4mm thick, using a mandolin if you have one (alternatively slice them by hand, using a sharp knife).

2. Sift the flour into a large bowl, then add the baking powder, salt and pepper and combine.

3. Slowly add the cold water to the bowl and whisk until there are no lumps and you have a smooth batter.

4. Pour enough oil into a frying pan to generously cover the base and bring to a medium heat (if it's too hot, the batter will burn before the courgettes are cooked through). You will need to constantly add more oil in small amounts as it gets absorbed.

5. Test a small pea-sized piece of batter in the oil, and if it turns golden in around a minute, the oil is ready. Line a large tray with kitchen paper.

6. Coat a slice of courgette in the batter, using a fork. Let any excess drip off for a few seconds, then carefully place in the pan. Repeat until the pan is full, and cook the courgettes on each side for around 2–3 minutes. Once cooked, place on the lined tray to drain any excess oil, then repeat until all the batter is used up.

7. Sprinkle with more sea salt and black pepper, and a light squeeze of lemon juice.

These little Italian rice balls take a while to make but are absolutely worth it and can be frozen for months. Nonna would whip up hundreds of these a week in the restaurant, filled with her bolognese sauce – but arancini can be filled with whatever you like. We've got two of our personal favourites below: a traditional plant-based mince and a creamy cavolo nero pesto that turns the rice a vibrant green. I developed the pesto arancini for my sold-out restaurant residence at Sicilian restaurant Norma, alongside the head chef, Giovann Attard.

ARANCINI
Classic Risotto Balls

MAKES: *8–10*
PREP TIME: *30 mins*
COOKING TIME: *30 mins*

INGREDIENTS ◆

1 vegetable stock cube
400g arborio rice
¼ tsp ground turmeric
1 stalk of celery
2 banana shallots
1–2 carrots
2 cloves of garlic
2 tbsp olive oil
350–500g plant-based
   mince
2 x 400g tins of chopped
   tomatoes
1 tsp salt
a pinch of chilli flakes
1 tbsp sugar
¼ tsp bicarbonate
   of soda
200g frozen peas
vegetable oil

Coating
250g Tipo 00 flour
400ml water
300g fine breadcrumbs

1. In a large saucepan, bring 900ml of water to the boil with 1 tablespoon of salt and 1 veg stock cube. Nonna's ratio is 1 part rice to 2 parts water (any cup will do for measuring). So you need 900ml of water for 400g of rice.

2. Add the arborio rice and cook according to the packet instructions, stirring every few minutes.

3. Stir in ¼ teaspoon of turmeric (you can use saffron if you like, in which case use a small pinch soaked in 30ml of water).

4. Once the rice is cooked, pour it on to a large tray and let it cool completely.

5. Now prepare the soffritto (a fancy name for celery, shallots and carrots). Chop them all finely – if you have a small food processor, use that, otherwise by hand is fine, it just takes longer! Finely slice the garlic.

6. In a large pan, heat the olive oil over a medium heat. Add the sliced garlic and the soffritto mixture and sauté for about 5 minutes, until softened.

7. Put a drizzle of oil into a separate pan and bring to a medium heat, then add the plant-based mince and cook for 5–10 minutes, until it's broken down and slightly browned. Add the mince to the softened veg.

»

8. Blend the tinned tomatoes using a hand blender (or regular blender) and pour into the pan along with ½ can's worth of water. Bring to a simmer and stir in the salt, chilli flakes, sugar and bicarbonate of soda (don't put too much bicarb in or you'll ruin the dish – it should bubble for 30 seconds, then disappear). Season to taste, then add the frozen peas and let the sauce simmer for about 20–30 minutes, stirring occasionally.

9. Drain the cooked mince mixture through a sieve over a bowl, saving the sauce to pour on top of the arancini later or to serve with pasta.

10. Now assemble your arancini. Once the rice has cooled, using wet hands, take a handful and flatten it in your hand. Place 1–2 tablespoons of the mince in the centre, and press between your hands to form a tight ball of rice, enclosing the mince. Add more rice if necessary, to seal it. Place on a lined tray, repeat with the rest of the mince and rice, then chill the balls for 30 minutes in the fridge.

11. Meanwhile, prepare the breadcrumb batter. Mix the flour with the water to create the *pastella*, which should resemble a batter mix in consistency. Spread the dried breadcrumbs on a large tray. Line a large plate with kitchen paper.

12. After the arancini balls have cooled for 30 minutes in the fridge, use a large slotted spoon to dip each one first into the batter mix and then into the dried breadcrumbs.

13. Heat 6–8 inches of vegetable oil for deep-frying in a large pot to 180°C and fry the arancini in batches until they are golden and crispy. This should take about 3–4 minutes per batch. Remove them using a slotted spoon and place them on the kitchen paper to remove excess oil.

14. Serve the arancini hot, with a side of marinara sauce or your favourite dipping sauce.

TIPS ◆

If you really want perfectly shaped arancini, you can pop them into the freezer for about 20 minutes after moulding. This will help them keep their shape when you dip them into the batter and breadcrumbs.

You can also use an arancini mould.

ARANCINI AL PESTO
Pesto-Stuffed Risotto Balls

MAKES: *8–10*
PREP TIME: *30 mins*
COOKING TIME: *30 mins*

INGREDIENTS ◆

about 1.3 litres vegetable stock

500g arborio rice

80g plant-based butter

100g plant-based cream cheese (e.g. Nush or Philadelphia)

20g cashew Parmesan (page 28)

1½ tsp salt

250g vegan mozzarella, grated

Coating

225g Tipo 00 flour

400ml water

300g breadcrumbs

vegetable oil, for frying

Kale pesto

150g green kale or cavolo nero

50g fresh basil leaves

1 small clove of garlic

3 tsp raw pumpkin seeds

zest of ½ a lemon

a pinch of salt

8 tbsp extra virgin olive oil

1. Remove the tough stems from the kale or cavolo nero and put the leaves into a food processor. Add the rest of the pesto ingredients and blitz until it forms a paste, adding more oil if needed. Set aside.

2. Put the veg stock into a large saucepan over a medium-high heat and bring to the boil.

3. Heat 2 tablespoons of oil in a separate large pan, then toast the rice for 2 minutes, stirring. Add the veg stock one ladle at a time, stirring continuously and only adding more once it has been absorbed. After about 15–20 minutes, when the rice is almost fully cooked but still has a little bite, stir through the plant-based butter and cream cheese, cashew Parmesan, kale pesto and salt. Remove from the heat.

4. Pour your rice mix on to a large tray (or divide between two) and let cool to room temperature, which should take about 30 minutes.

5. Once the rice mix has cooled, use wet hands to form it into balls, about 120g each. Stuff each ball with 15g of vegan mozzarella (a heaped teaspoon) and press it between your hands to form a cone shape. Place on a lined tray, repeat with the rest of the rice and filling, then chill the balls for 30 minutes in the fridge.

6. Meanwhile, prepare the coating. Mix the flour with the water to create the pastella, which should resemble a batter mix in consistency. Spread the dried breadcrumbs on a large tray.

7. After the arancini have cooled, use a large slotted spoon to dip each one first into the batter mix and then into the breadcrumbs.

8. Heat 6–8 inches of vegetable oil for deep-frying in a large pot to 180°C and fry the arancini in batches until they are golden and crispy. This should take about 3–4 minutes per batch. Remove them using a slotted spoon and place them on kitchen paper to remove excess oil.

9. Serve with a sprinkle of vegan Parmesan (this is absolutely not traditional but tastes delicious) and a pinch of salt.

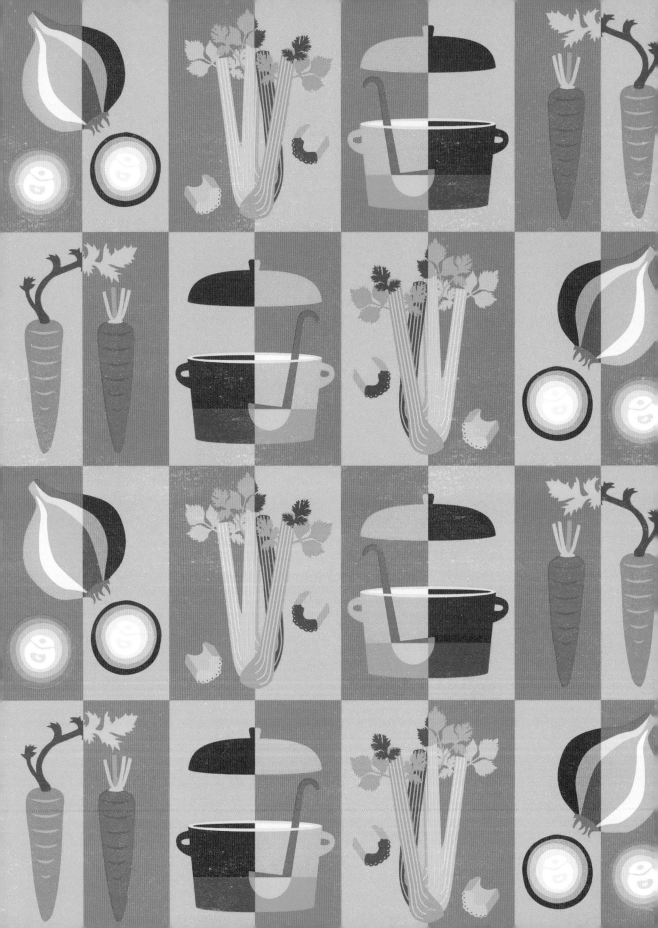

ZUPPE E MINESTRE
Soups & Stews

Nonna's hearty minestra is perfect for those cold winter nights or for when you're feeling a bit under the weather – it's essentially a vegetable soup, but with a bit of Italian oomph. Every nonna has a different minestra recipe, but this is the one I grew up with. I love the etymology of the word minestra – meaning 'soup', or more literally, 'that which is served', from minestrare, 'to serve' and cognate with administer as in 'to administer a remedy'.

NONNA'S MINESTRA
Hearty Vegetable Soup

SERVES: *3-4*
PREP TIME: *10 mins*
COOKING TIME: *30 mins*

INGREDIENTS ◆

4 carrots
1 white onion
1 potato
1 leek
2 stalks celery
¼ of a green cabbage
½ a head of broccoli
olive oil
20g plant-based butter
1 x 400g tin of tomatoes (optional)
100g peas
1 veg stock cube

1. Finely chop the vegetables into cubes. If you're feeling lazy, you can blitz them in a food processor to save time. Heat the oil and butter on a medium heat in a large saucepan, and once the butter has melted, add the vegetables and sauté for 5 minutes.

2. When the vegetables are soft, add the tinned tomatoes and enough hot water to cover the veg. Crumble in 1 stock cube and season with salt and pepper to taste (you can add a pinch of chilli flakes here if you like spice, which I absolutely don't).

3. Simmer for 15–20 minutes, adding the peas in the last 5 minutes.

4. Serve your minestra with fresh bread, or with my homemade vegan focaccia on page 100.

TIPS ◆

Not only is this soup-er healthy, you can also keep it in your freezer for weeks and reheat it whenever you need a quick dinner.

Nonna's supergreen soup, aka zuppa di spinaci, is similar to minestra, but I find it has a much deeper and richer flavour due to the bags of spinach required! This is a nutritional powerhouse packed with iron, fibre, calcium and vitamin C, plus it's a great way to use up a bunch of greens. It also freezes really well, so it's the perfect healthy meal to have a few portions of for those cold winter nights.

ZUPPA DI SPINACI
Nonna's Supergreen Soup

SERVES: 4–6
PREP TIME: 6 mins
COOKING TIME: 20 mins

INGREDIENTS ◆

4 tbsp extra virgin olive oil

100g vegan butter (or extra olive oil)

3 leeks

2 white onions

3 stalks of celery

1 head of broccoli

2 carrots

500g fresh spinach

1 veg stock cube

1 tablespoon of salt

½ tsp chilli flakes

vegan single cream, to serve

NONNA'S TOP TIP ◆

Before chopping the leek, make a slice about two-thirds down and open it up under a running tap to wash out any dirt or bugs.

1. Put the olive oil and butter into a large saucepan. If you don't want to use butter, simply add a bit of extra oil.

2. Chop all the vegetables. It doesn't matter too much how they are all chopped, as the soup gets blended, but Nonna likes to dice the onions, cut the carrots into small 2cm chunks, cut the celery and leeks into 1cm discs, and chop the broccoli into small florets. Don't throw away the stems – Nonna says these are *più gustosi*, which means they have more flavour, so throw them in too!

3. Add all the chopped veg to the pan of butter and oil, place over a medium-high heat, and stir for a few minutes to evenly coat all the veg. Let it cook for 5–10 minutes.

4. Meanwhile, fill and boil the kettle, and wash your giant amount of spinach.

5. After the veg has begun to soften, add the washed spinach and pour in about 1½–2 litres of hot water from the kettle – you want it to just about reach the top of the veg.

6. Add the veg stock cube, 1 tablespoon of salt and a ½ teaspoon of chilli flakes, and mix well until the stock cube dissolves.

7. Pop the lid on and let the soup simmer for a further 10–15 minutes. Then it's time to blend! (You can leave it as is if you prefer a chunkier soup.)

8. Once blended, serve with a drizzle of cream, some warm crusty bread and a sprinkle of Parmesan, if you like.

A ribollita is somewhere between a soup and a stew. Originating in Tuscany but enjoyed all over Italy, this hearty one-pot dish is super nutritious, cheap to make and a great way of using up stale bread. Traditionally you would put a leftover rind from a Parmesan in the soup, so I've added a touch of nutritional yeast to give it a hint of cheesy flavour.

RIBOLLITA
Tuscan Bread Soup

SERVES: *6*
PREP TIME: *15 mins*
COOKING TIME: *40 mins*

INGREDIENTS ◆

3 tbsp extra virgin olive oil, plus extra for drizzling

1 small white onion

2 stalks of celery

2 small carrots

4 cloves of garlic

1 tbsp tomato purée

1 tsp fennel seeds

½ tsp chilli flakes

1.2 litres vegetable stock, or 2 veg stock cubes

1 x 400g tin of chopped tomatoes

1 tbsp fresh rosemary, finely chopped

2 tbsp nutritional yeast

salt and black pepper

1 x 400g tin of cannellini beans

200g cavolo nero

150g Savoy cabbage or Chinese cabbage

125g stale crusty bread (a sourdough or ciabatta works best)

grated vegan Parmesan

1. Put the olive oil into a large casserole dish over a medium heat. Finely slice the onion, chop the celery and carrots, and add them to the pot. Fry for 10–15 minutes on a medium-high heat until the onion is golden and the veg is all soft. Crush the garlic and add to the pan with the tomato purée, fennel seeds and chilli flakes. Continue to fry, while stirring, for a further 2 minutes.

2. If using veg stock cubes, dissolve them in 1.2 litres of hot water. Pour the veg stock and chopped tomatoes into the pan, followed by the chopped rosemary and nutritional yeast. Season with salt and black pepper and leave to bubble and reduce for 25 minutes.

3. Meanwhile, drain and rinse the cannellini beans and add two-thirds of them to the soup. Place the rest of the beans in a small bowl and, using the back of a fork, mash them into a paste. Stir this paste through the soup – this adds a creaminess and helps thicken it.

4. Remove the thick stems from the cavolo nero and roughly chop the leaves. Chop the cabbage, avoiding the stalk, and stir both through the soup. Leave to simmer for 1–2 minutes.

5. Season to taste. If the soup is looking too thick and stew-like and you want more liquid, add a splash more stock.

6. Finally, tear the stale bread into bite-size chunks. Add them to the soup, and serve in bowls with a good drizzle of extra virgin olive oil and some vegan Parmesan. By the time you're ready to eat, the bread will be soft and will have absorbed all the flavours of the soup.

This is a typical *cucina povera* dish which is made around St Joseph's Day. When I visited Sicily to shoot some of this book, we asked all of Nonna's sisters to contribute one dish, and Zia Felicina, who grew up alongside Nonna in Sicily, made this. She explained the history of the dish as something all the neighbours get involved in, contributing different ingredients and scraps of pasta. What is special about this soup is that each family and village will have their own unique recipe for it, but this one belongs to my Zia Felicina.

MINESTRA DI SAN GIUSEPPE
St Joseph's Soup

SERVES: *4–6*
PREP TIME: *overnight*
COOKING TIME: *1–2 hours*

INGREDIENTS ◆

250g dried borlotti beans

100g dried broad beans

250g dried green lentils

3 stalks of celery

1 large white onion

100g cherry tomatoes

¼ of a fennel bulb (approx. 150g) or a handful of wild fennel stalks

salt and black pepper

1 vegetable stock cube

85g angel hair or capellini

85g maltagliati or broken lasagne sheets

85g ditalini or any small hoop pasta

extra virgin olive oil

chopped fresh parsley, to serve

1. Soak all the dried beans and lentils in a large bowl filled with water for 2–6 hours, depending on how big they are. If you're using giant broad beans, these are best soaked overnight, but for regular ones 2 hours is fine. Replace the water every 2 hours (or at least twice).

2. Once soaked, rinse the beans in clean water, making sure to remove all the foam that comes off, then put them into the largest saucepan you can find and fill it up with water to about 10cm above the beans. Bring the beans to a low simmer for 2–3 hours, or until the largest beans can be mashed with two fingers. You will need to keep adding water throughout this recipe, making sure it never goes down to the level of the beans.

3. Meanwhile, prepare all the vegetables: slice the celery into 1cm discs, finely slice the onion, and halve the cherry tomatoes. Finely chop the fennel.

4. Once the beans are soft, add all the chopped vegetables and the fennel along with 1 tablespoon of salt, and crumble in the veg stock cube.

5. Stir well and bring to a low simmer for 8–10 minutes, then break up the pasta and add to the pan. Add more water if needed, and continue to cook for a further 8–10 minutes, until the pasta is al dente. If you are using different kinds of pasta, make sure to put

»

You need around 250–300g pasta in total – a mix of whatever you have, but Zia likes a mix of maltagliati n.66, ditalini n.26 and spaghetti n.5 (thin).

This will freeze well!

the one that takes the longest in first. Stir occasionally to prevent any pasta sticking to the bottom.

6. Reduce the heat and add more water if needed, as it will get slightly thicker as it cools. Season to taste with salt and pepper, and serve with a good drizzle of extra virgin olive oil and a sprinkling of chopped fresh parsley.

PANE
Bread

There's really nothing quite like the smell of fresh bread filling your kitchen, and these miscati are no exception. The trick is to roll and twist them in a specific way so that it's less of a stuffed doughnut shape and more of an inverted ribbon. This results in the filling being evenly distributed and the bread being nice and crunchy on the outside yet soft and fluffy on the inside.

MISCATI
Olive Bread Rolls

MAKES: *10–12*
PREP TIME: *1 hour 30 mins*
COOKING TIME: *40 mins*

INGREDIENTS ◆

500g strong wholemeal bread flour

200g strong white bread flour

1 x 7g sachet of instant yeast

½ tbsp sugar

1 tsp fine salt

½ tbsp olive oil, plus extra for kneading and drizzling

560ml lukewarm water

1 large banana shallot or 1 small white onion

200g pitted black olives

salt and black pepper

100g grated vegan Parmesan (optional)

1. Combine the flour, yeast and sugar in the bowl of a stand mixer fitted with a dough hook. Give it a quick mix, then add the salt.

2. With the mixer running on slow, gradually pour in the olive oil and lukewarm water until it all combines into a sticky dough.

3. Turn the mixer speed up to medium and leave it to knead for 10 minutes, by which time your dough should be elastic and smooth.

4. Lightly oil a large mixing bowl and put in the dough. Cover with a damp cloth and leave somewhere warm until the dough has doubled in size (approximately 1 hour, but it depends how cold your house is).

5. While you wait for the dough to rise, tidy up, go for a walk, then finely chop the shallot or onion and place in a small bowl. Add a pinch of salt and pepper. Prep your olives if you need to pit them – but I'd recommend buying ready pitted ones in oil.

6. Preheat the oven to 180°C fan/200°C and grease and line two large baking trays with olive oil and parchment paper.

7. Once the dough has risen, transfer it on to a cloth and divide it into 2 equal pieces. Set one piece aside.

8. Spread 2 tablespoons of olive oil over your work surface and place one piece of dough on it. Knock the air out of the dough by kneading it for 10 seconds, until all pockets of air have been removed. Roll the dough lengthways to form a sausage shape, then push it down to form a rectangle approximately 60cm by 10cm, with the long edge towards you.

»

9. Drizzle over a good, and I mean *good*, glug of olive oil, and spread half the shallots or onions and half the olives evenly along the length of the dough. Scatter over half the vegan Parmesan and again drizzle generously with olive oil – don't be shy! Imagine Nonna is looking over your shoulder saying more, more, more!

10. Starting with the long edge of the dough nearest you, roll it up over the filling until you reach halfway. Then take the top edge and roll it down over the top half of the dough, to meet in the middle. I can imagine this is kind of like rolling a giant cigarette, but made of bread and stuffed with olives.

11. Using a sharp knife, cut the rolled-up dough into 6 even pieces, each approximately 10cm long.

12. Pick up the first piece then, using the palms of your hands, cup the dough gently and shape it into a round ball with a flat bottom. Place on one of the lined baking trays, and repeat with the 5 remaining pieces of dough, leaving at least 5cm between each one as they will expand as they rise. Cover the tray with a damp tea towel.

13. Repeat steps 8–12 with the second half of the dough and place on the second lined oven tray.

14. Bake in the preheated oven for 30–40 minutes, until golden. If you are unsure whether they are cooked, carefully pick one up and look underneath. The base should be nice and golden, and if you give it a tap, it will sound hollow.

TIPS ◆

One thing I never liked was how Nonna always used olives that still had the pits in because apparently they taste better, but I can't tell you how many times I've almost broken a tooth biting into one of those rock-solid olives – so I'd highly recommend pitting the olives beforehand or, to make your life even easier, using pitted olives!

You can store these in the freezer for weeks: just let them cool down first, then pop them into freezer bags. To defrost, simply pop them into the oven at 180°C fan/200°C for 10–15 minutes!

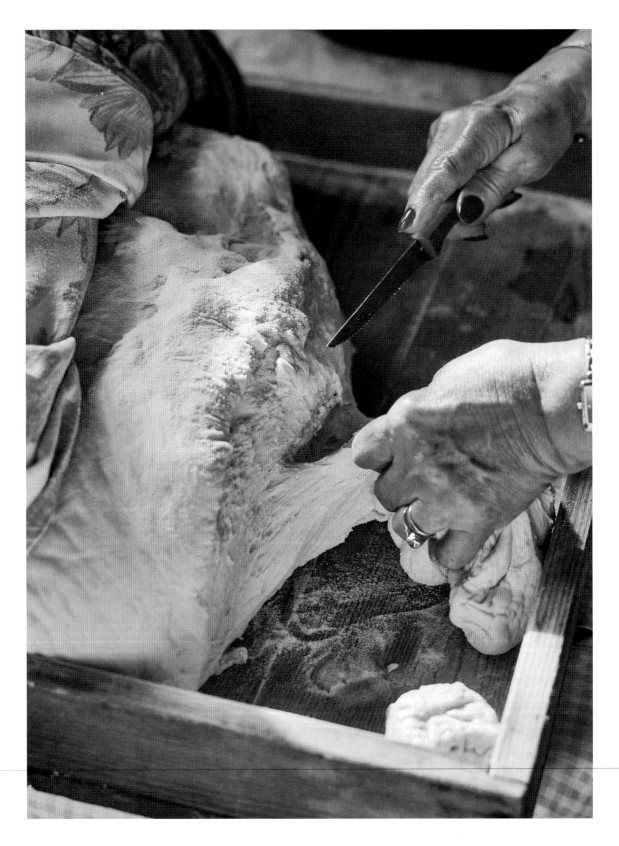

Nonna
APPROVED

There's nothing like the smell of homemade focaccia and it can be a labour of love but Nonna's version is super simple. We like to enjoy it topped with fresh cherry tomatoes and rosemary. The key to great focaccia is great olive oil, so try to use a rich, deep-coloured variety for the most authentic taste and texture.

FOCACCIA

SERVES: *4*
PREP TIME: *2–3 hours*
COOKING TIME: *15 mins*

INGREDIENTS ◆

500g strong bread flour
1 tsp caster sugar
1 tbsp fast action yeast
2 tsp fine salt
40ml extra virgin olive oil, plus extra for shaping and drizzling
250–300ml lukewarm water
150g cherry tomatoes
olives
4 sprigs fresh rosemary
sea salt flakes

TIPS ◆

Make sure to use lukewarm water. If the water is too hot, it will kill the yeast and the bread won't rise as well!

You can make this by hand – just follow step 1 but use a large bowl instead, then stir with a wooden spoon until a shaggy dough forms and knead on an oiled work surface for 10 minutes.

1. Put the flour, sugar and yeast into the bowl of a stand mixer, fitted with a dough hook, and stir on a low setting for 30 seconds. Once combined, with the mixer running, add the fine salt and olive oil, then gradually add the warm water and continue mixing until a sticky dough forms. You may not need all the water.

2. Raise the mixer speed to medium and leave to knead for 8–10 minutes, until the dough is elastic and coming away from the sides. Cover the bowl with cling film or a damp cloth and leave in a warm room to rise until it has doubled in size (usually 1–2 hours).

3. While the dough rises, grease a deep baking tray or roasting tin, roughly 20 x 30cm, with 2 tablespoons of olive oil, making sure to cover all the sides of the tray to prevent your focaccia from sticking. Preheat the oven to 220°C/200°C fan.

4. When the dough has doubled in size, place it on your oiled tray and, pushing it with your fingertips, stretch it out to the size of the tray. Let the dough rest for another 45 minutes to an hour, or until it has puffed up again.

5. Spreading your fingers wide, gently press dimples into the dough roughly 4cm apart. Add the cherry tomatoes, olives and rosemary into the dimples and over the dough, being careful not to deflate it as you do. Drizzle over a generous amount of olive oil and scatter with flaky sea salt.

6. Bake for 20–25 minutes, until pillowy and golden brown. Remove from the tray and cool on a rack.

Pizza is quite possibly the most quintessential Italian food – and Nonna's version is a take on a typical Sicilian pizza, otherwise known as sfincione. It's closer to a deep-dish style pizza with a thick crust, and is light and fluffy. Make a batch of Nonna's tomato sauce (page 124) and use that as the base, then simply top with your favourite ingredients – Nonna likes olives, artichokes and mozzarella. We shot this in Sicily with all of Nonna's sisters and even managed to squeeze them all into my Zio's classic Fiat 500.

NONNA'S PIZZA

MAKES: *2–4 small pizzas*
PREP TIME: *2 hours 10 mins*
COOKING TIME: *10 mins*

INGREDIENTS ◆

500g white bread flour or Tipo 00 flour

1 tsp sugar

1 x 7g sachet of instant yeast

¾ tbsp fine salt

350ml tepid water

extra virgin olive oil, for greasing

1. Put the flour into the bowl of a stand mixer fitted with a dough hook. (If making by hand, add to a large bowl.) Add the sugar and yeast and mix slowly for 10 seconds, then add the salt and mix briefly again.

2. Slowly add the water until a dough starts to form, then turn the mixer up to medium and leave to knead for 6–8 minutes, until the dough is smooth and elastic. (Knead by hand on a lightly floured surface for 8–10 minutes until smooth.)

3. Cover the bowl of the mixer with cling film or a tea towel and leave for 1–2 hours, or until the dough has doubled in size.

4. With oiled hands, tip the dough out on to a lightly floured work surface and cut into two equal halves, then let them rest for 10 minutes.

5. Once rested, shape each half into a round dough ball, then gently stretch it outwards, pushing from the centre with your fingers until you have about a 25cm circle.

6. Preheat the oven to 230°C fan/250°C. If using a pizza oven, preheat it to 300°C.

7. Top your pizza with Nonna's tomato sauce (see page 124), vegan cheese and your favourite toppings, then cook in a pizza oven for 2–4 minutes or a conventional oven for 8–12 minutes.

Freshly made bread is one of life's great joys – and Nonna's is no exception. I have fond memories of walking into her kitchen and seeing tea towels everywhere with odd-looking lumps in them, only to peek underneath and discover fresh dough about to go into the oven!

PANE DI NONNA
Nonna's Bread

MAKESS: *4 small loaves*
PREP TIME: *2 hours*
COOKING TIME: *35 mins*

INGREDIENTS ◆

500g strong white bread flour

50g fine semolina flour

¾ tbsp caster sugar

1 x 7g sachet of instant yeast

¾ tbsp fine salt

350ml tepid water

35ml olive oil

To coat
25ml plant-based milk
50g sesame seeds

1. Put both flours into the bowl of a stand mixer fitted with a dough hook. Add the sugar and yeast and mix slowly for 10 seconds, then add the salt and mix briefly again. Add the water and mix until a dough starts to form. Add the oil and mix again. Turn the mixer up to medium and leave to knead for 6–8 minutes, until the dough is smooth and elastic.

2. Cover the bowl of the mixer with a tea towel and leave for 1–2 hours, or until the dough has doubled in size.

3. Tip the dough out on to a lightly floured work surface and knead briefly to knock the air out of it. Divide into 4 even-sized pieces and form into whichever shape you like – a plait, a bun or a simple breadstick. Nonna likes to make a *pesciolino*, which is a fish shape. Transfer the dough shapes to a large baking sheet lined with baking paper.

4. Cover with a tea towel and leave for another 30 minutes.

5. Meanwhile, preheat the oven to 190°C fan/210°C.

6. Brush the loaves gently with plant-based milk, sprinkle with sesame seeds, and make a few slashes in the top with a knife.

7. Place in the oven for 30–35 minutes, until golden brown and the loaves sound hollow when you tap them on the bottom.

8. Turn the oven off, open the door and leave for 10 minutes.

9. Remove the loaves from the oven and leave them to cool on a rack for 10–15 minutes, then serve warm and sliced, with olive oil, salt and pepper. Alternatively you can let the loaves cool and freeze them.

Sweet brioche filled with a big dollop of soft gelato – a common breakfast on hot summer days in Sicily. You might think it's odd to have ice cream in a bun, but trust me, a waffle could never.

BRIOCHES VEGANA
Vegan Brioche

MAKES: *8 buns*
PREP TIME: *3 hours*
COOKING TIME: *15 mins*

INGREDIENTS ◆

125g vegan butter

175g plant-based milk

375g plain flour

65g caster sugar

1 x 7g sachet of instant yeast

½ tsp fine salt

1 tsp vanilla paste or vanilla extract

Glaze

2 tbsp plant-based milk

2 tbsp maple syrup or agave syrup

1. Dice the vegan butter into roughly 1cm cubes and set aside to soften. Pour the plant-based milk into a small saucepan and place over a low heat until the milk is lukewarm (approximately body temperature). Remove from the heat and set aside.

2. Place the flour, caster sugar and yeast in the bowl of a stand mixer fitted with a paddle attachment. Turn the machine on and mix on medium for 30 seconds to combine everything. Then add the salt.

3. With the machine still running on medium, slowly pour in the lukewarm plant milk and vanilla. Then, as the flour mixes in and a dough begins to form, start adding the cubes of softened butter a few at a time.

4. Once the butter is all added, leave the dough to knead for 10 minutes until it forms a smooth ball and has come away from the sides of the bowl.

5. Cover the bowl with cling film or a damp tea towel and leave to prove at room temperature until doubled in size. This usually takes 2–3 hours but it will depend on how warm the room is.

6. Once the dough has risen, tip it on to a lightly floured work surface and knead briefly to knock all the air out of it.

7. Optionally, cut a roughly 50g piece of dough and set aside – this will be used for the small balls of dough that sit on top of each brioche.

8. Divide the rest of the dough into 8 equal pieces.

»

9. Make sure the work surface is still lightly floured, then take one piece of dough and shape it into a round ball. Place on a large, lined baking tray. Repeat with the remaining dough and add to the tray, making sure to space them out well as they will expand as they prove. If you don't have a really big oven tray, divide them between two lined trays.

10. If adding a small ball on top for the authentic sicilian style, take the remaining 50g piece of dough and divide it into 8. Take one small piece and shape it into a small ball. Using your index finger, gently press an indent into the top of one of the large buns on the tray and press the small ball on top. Repeat with the remaining buns.

11. Cover the tray with a damp tea towel and set aside for another hour, or until the buns have doubled in size.

12. Meanwhile, preheat the oven to 170°C fan/190°C.

13. In a small bowl mix together the plant milk and maple syrup for the glaze. Using a pastry brush, gently brush the glaze over the tops of the buns.

14. Place in the preheated oven and bake for 12–14 minutes, until the buns are golden and puffed up. If the buns look like they are getting too brown too quickly, cover them loosely with kitchen foil.

15. Remove from the oven and transfer the buns to a wire rack to cool completely before eating.

TIP ◆

If you want the buns to be really shiny and glossy, brush them with a little more maple syrup or agave syrup when they come out of the oven.

PASTA
Pasta

Nonna
APPROVED

This is an all-round recipe that will work both for different types of pasta shapes and for rolling sheets of pasta for dishes like lasagne, tortellini and tagliatelle. The turmeric is optional but gives the dough a lovely yellow colour, more like a fresh egg pasta. Semolina flour (*semola rimacinata*) is available from Italian delis and some supermarkets, and is easily found online.

PASTA FRESCA VEGANA
Homemade Vegan Pasta

SERVES: *4*
PREP TIME: *1 hour and 15 mins*
COOKING TIME: *10 mins*

INGREDIENTS ◆

250g fine semolina flour (*semola rimacinata*)

150g Tipo 00 flour

1 tsp fine salt

¼ tsp ground turmeric (optional)

225ml warm water

2 tsp olive oil

1. In a large bowl, combine both types of flour, the salt and the turmeric (if using). Tip it on to a work surface (you can also do this in the bowl if it's big enough, which is slightly less messy). Make a well in the centre and pour in the warm water and olive oil.

2. Using your fingers, gradually incorporate the water into the flour until everything is combined and you have a dough.

3. Knead the dough for around 10 minutes, until it is smooth and elastic. Wrap the ball of dough in cling film and put it in the fridge to rest for at least an hour before rolling.

If you want to impress a date, a friend or, heck, even your nan, this is a show-stopping recipe that's a labour of love but absolutely worth it. Making your own pasta from scratch can be daunting but I promise it's actually not that difficult! I'd recommend getting a pasta machine – you can pick one up for about £30 and it's a great addition to a kitchen if you love pasta!

RAVIOLI VERDI CON NOCI E CREMA DI FUNGHI

Green Ravioli with Walnut Stuffing & Mushroom Cream

SERVES: *4*
PREP TIME: *45 mins*
COOKING TIME: *15 mins*

INGREDIENTS ◆

Pasta dough
200g spinach
125ml cold water
150g fine semolina
175g Tipo 00 flour
1 tbsp olive oil

For the walnut filling
100g toasted walnuts
15g fresh basil
½ a clove of garlic
extra virgin olive oil
150g plant-based cream cheese
salt and pepper

Mushroom cream
250ml mushroom stock (15g dried porcini soaked in 250ml hot water with a pinch of salt)
150ml soy milk
25g vegan butter
25g Tipo 00 flour

1. Start by making the ravioli dough. Bring a pan of water to the boil with a good pinch of salt. Add the spinach and cook for 30 seconds just until it has wilted. Remove, squeeze it nice and tight, then run it under cold water before squeezing again to remove as much water as you can.

2. Using a hand blender or mini blender, blitz the blanched spinach with the 125ml of cold water, until a very smooth purée is formed.

3. Put the spinach purée and the rest of the ingredients for the pasta dough into a food processor or mixer and mix until the dough leaves the sides and is no longer sticky to touch.

4. Knead the dough on a floured surface for 10 minutes, until it's nice and smooth – it may look dry to start with, but keep going!

5. Rest the dough for at least half an hour in the fridge, covered with cling film.

6. Roughly chop the walnuts for the filling and the garnish, and grate the garlic.

7. For the filling, pulse the walnuts, basil, garlic and olive oil in a food processor or finely chop by hand. Put the cream cheese into a separate small bowl, give it a loose mix on its own, then stir through the pulsed walnut and basil mix until well incorporated. Season to taste and set aside.

»

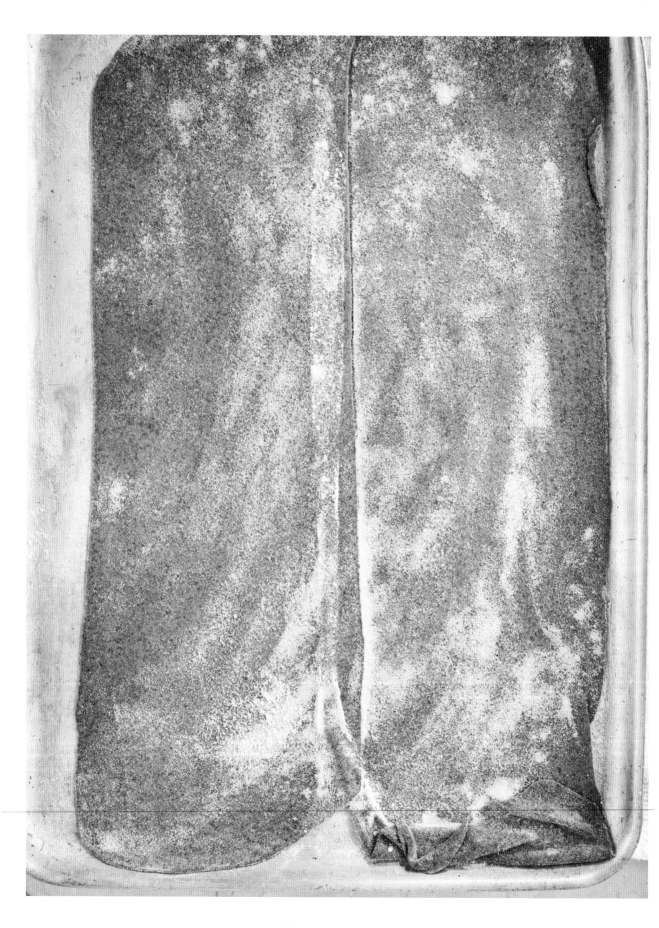

Garnish
100g king oyster or
  woodland mushrooms
10g toasted walnuts
5g fresh tarragon
olive oil, for drizzling

8. Cut the dough into 4 equal pieces, then roll each one into a rectangle on a floured surface to approx. 2mm thick. This is much easier with a pasta machine, but absolutely doable by hand too!

9. Pipe or spoon 1 teaspoon of filling in a line along 2 of the pieces of dough, with at least 4cm gap each side. Lightly brush the area around each mound with water or plant-based milk, then gently lay a second sheet of pasta on top of each, pressing around each mound with your fingers to seal them in nice and snug.

10. Cut the pasta into squares between the mounds of filling using a sharp knife, or a wheel cutter if you have one, and place on a tray.

11. For the mushroom cream, blend the porcini mushrooms along with the water they soaked in to form a smooth liquid, then pour this into a small saucepan, add the soy milk and heat until warm.

12. In a separate saucepan, melt the butter over a low heat. Add the flour and whisk for 1–2 minutes, then gradually pour in the warmed mushroom mix from the other saucepan, whisking continuously. Once you have a smooth sauce, bring it to a simmer and bubble for 3–4 minutes until it becomes a thick, silky sauce. Season well with salt and pepper.

13. Cut the oyster mushrooms into slices and sauté in a little oil until nice and brown.

14. Meanwhile, cook the ravioli in salted boiling water for 3–4 minutes.

15. To serve, spoon the mushroom cream over the base of a plate, layer on the pasta, and top with the sautéed mushrooms, toasted walnuts and tarragon. Finish with a drizzle of olive oil and enjoy.

TIP ◆
You need a small blender or stick blender to make the purée for this pasta shape. If you don't have one, why not try my simple scissor-cut pasta shape on page 129 instead?

Nonna
APPROVED

This is quite possibly the single most important recipe in this book. There's nothing quite like Nonna's pasta sauce – it's smooth, rich, balanced, and is the perfect sauce for any lasagne or bolognese, or simply for your favourite pasta. I grew up fortunate enough to eat this every Sunday minimum in Nonna's kitchen. We would visit for dinner, and as soon as we walked in we could smell the sweetness of the tomato sauce in the air.

NONNA'S SUGO DI POMODORO

Nonna's Pasta with Tomato Sauce

SERVES: *4*
PREP TIME: *10 mins*
COOKING TIME: *30 mins*

INGREDIENTS ◆

2–3 cloves of garlic

1 small carrot

2 small sweet banana shallots

3 tbsp good-quality olive oil

2 x 400g tins of chopped tomatoes

¼–½ tsp bicarbonate of soda

a pinch of chilli flakes

1½ tsp salt

1–2 tsp sugar

vegan Parmesan cheese, to serve (optional)

fresh basil, to serve (optional)

1. Finely chop the garlic, carrot and shallots.

2. Fry all the chopped vegetables in olive oil on a medium heat for 10 minutes, until softened.

3. Add the tinned tomatoes and one tin's worth of water, stir well and bring to a soft boil.

4. Once boiling, add the chilli flakes, salt, sugar and bicarbonate of soda. Stir well, it should bubble for 30 seconds, keep stirring and then reduce the heat to a very low simmer for 20–30 minutes.

5. Meanwhile, bring a large pan of water to the boil, add a pinch of salt (it should taste like sea water), then add your pasta of choice.

6. After 20–30 minutes, taste the sauce and season as necessary with more salt or chilli flakes, then use a hand blender to blitz it to a smooth texture.

7. Drain the pasta and transfer it to a large bowl.

8. This bit is important and is what makes the eating experience much more authentic and tasty – add a few spoonfuls of the sauce to the pasta in the large bowl and mix evenly, then serve with an extra few dollops of sauce on top.

9. If you like, top with vegan Parmesan and fresh basil.

This sauce freezes incredibly well, and I'd highly recommend making it in large batches and storing it in several Tupperware containers in the freezer. It will keep for 6 months easily, and can simply be defrosted on the hob or in the microwave, ready to be served with fresh pasta!

If you have some mushrooms lying around, you can chop a couple of them finely and add them to the sauce to give a subtle earthy taste.

If making fresh pasta sounds a bit scary, this is for you! It's practically foolproof, as you don't need any fancy equipment, just a pair of scissors. This technique actually originated in China but recently went viral on social media thanks to my good friend @seemagetsbaked. This recipe uses a tangy lemon and parsley sauce, but you can also try it with one of the pesto recipes on page 140.

CAVATELLI AGLI SPINACI
Kinda Cavatelli with Spinach

SERVES: *2–3*
PREP TIME: *10 mins*
COOKING TIME: *10 mins*

INGREDIENTS ◆

250g spinach

150–170g Tipo 00 flour

½ tsp salt

2 tbsp olive oil

2 cloves of garlic

30g fresh parsley

½ tsp chilli flakes

zest of 1 lemon

juice of ½ a lemon

3 tbsp vegan cream cheese (approx. 100g)

sea salt and black pepper

grated plant-based Parmesan or cashew Parmesan (see page 28), to serve

1. Blend the spinach, 150g of flour and the salt in a food processor until well combined. The mixture will look a bit grainy, but that's OK. If the dough is sticky to touch, add a touch more flour and blend again.

2. Remove the mixture to a floured surface and clump it all together with your hands, then knead for 2–3 minutes.

3. Bring a pan of water to the boil and season with salt. Then, using a pair of scissors, slice off thin, long pieces of the dough, approx. 5cm long and 1cm wide, and let them drop into the water.

4. Cook until al dente, which should take only about 2–5 minutes (they should float to the top when ready).

5. Meanwhile, slice the garlic and chop the parsley. Put 2 table-spoons of olive oil into a frying pan and place on a medium heat. Add the garlic and chilli flakes and stir to infuse the oil.

6. Add the parsley, lemon zest, lemon juice, cream cheese, salt and black pepper, and mix well to combine.

7. Transfer the cooked pasta to the pan and stir well, then cook for a further 1 minute so the liquid thickens up.

8. Serve immediately, topped with Parmesan and a pinch of black pepper.

Nonna
APPROVED

Pasta alla Norma, or pasta with aubergines, is a typical Sicilian pasta dish, originating in Catania, which just so happens to be naturally plant-based. Nonna and I made this on our first-ever live cooking segment on national TV with 2 million people watching. If it's good enough for Angela Hartnett and Matt Tebbutt, it's good enough for you!

PASTA ALLA NORMA
Pasta with Aubergines

SERVES: *2–3*
PREP TIME: *15 mins*
COOKING TIME: *30 mins*

INGREDIENTS ◆

2–3 large aubergines

2 cloves of garlic

2 x 400g tins of tomatoes

¼ tsp bicarbonate of soda

a pinch of sugar

salt and black pepper

3–4 fresh basil leaves, plus more to serve

olive oil, for the sauce

vegetable oil, for the aubergines

250g radiatori or penne pasta

vegan Parmesan, to serve

1. Peel the skin off the aubergines – it doesn't matter if some bits of skin remain, we're keeping it rustic just like Nonna does.

2. Cut the aubergines lengthways about 1cm thick. Place them in a bowl and cover with cold water, then add a generous amount of salt (about 1–2 tablespoons). Make sure the slices are all covered – you want to give them a salty bath for about 10 minutes.

3. Thinly slice the garlic and fry in olive oil on a medium heat for 1 minute, then add the tinned tomatoes along with 1 tin's worth of water and bring to a low simmer.

4. After 10 minutes of soaking, drain the aubergines, place them on a tea towel, and pat lightly to drain any remaining liquid.

5. Shallow fry the aubergine slices in a pan with veg oil over medium-high heat for 2–4 minutes each side until well coloured – you're looking for a deep brown. Once cooked, pop them on a plate lined with a piece of kitchen paper and repeat the process until they're all cooked – this will take a while, so be patient!

6. Once the tomato sauce is bubbling, add sugar, salt and pepper, tear in the basil leaves and bicarbonate of soda and stir then reduce the heat to a low simmer for 20 minutes.

7. Cook the pasta in salted water according to the packet instructions.

8. While the pasta is cooking, chop the aubergines into small chunks.

9. Once the pasta is cooked, transfer it directly to the pan of tomato sauce, then add the chopped aubergines and mix everything together. Serve with more fresh basil and grated Parmesan.

This is probably the quickest pasta recipe you'll ever make, as it only takes as long as the pasta takes to cook! I grew up with Nonna making this when there were large family gatherings. This recipe was the first video to 'blow up' on social media, reaching five million views – the population of Sicily – in under a week.

PASTA AGLIO, OLIO E PEPERONCINO

Pasta with Garlic, Oil & Chilli

SERVES: *4*
PREP TIME: *5 mins*
COOKING TIME: *10 mins*

INGREDIENTS ◆

1 tbsp fine salt

300g spaghetti

2–4 cloves of garlic (depending on who you're seeing the next day!)

a handful of fresh parsley

100ml olive oil

1 tsp chilli flakes

vegan Parmesan, to serve

1. Bring a pan of water to the boil, add 1 tbsp fine salt. Cook the spaghetti according to the packet instructions.

2. Meanwhile, crush the garlic and chop the parsley.

3. In a large pan on a very low heat, mix the olive oil, garlic, chilli flakes and parsley.

4. Drain the cooked pasta, reserving 1–2 cups of the cooking water.

5. Transfer the pasta to the pan and mix thoroughly, adding some of the pasta cooking water to coat to a silky consistency.

6. Serve into plates and top with lots of vegan Parmesan, or my homemade cashew Parmesan (see page 28).

TIPS ◆

Heating the garlic is entirely optional – with the right quantities this dish works just as well without heating it.

Taste and season as you go, but as long as you're using some sort of Parmesan alternative and the pasta water is salted well enough, there's no need to add any more salt!

Eating plant-based doesn't mean you have to miss out on juicy meatballs, and this tempeh version is tried and tested on Nonna herself and she loved it! Tempeh is like tofu's less popular cousin – it's higher in protein, has a meatier texture and absorbs flavour really well, which makes for a great ingredient in the plant-based meatballs. These are delicious served with Nonna's pasta sauce.

SPAGHETTI CON POLPETTE
Pasta with Homemade Tempeh Meatballs

SERVES: *3–4*
PREP TIME: *40 mins*
COOKING TIME: *20 mins*

INGREDIENTS ◆

1 heaped tbsp ground flaxseed

½ small white onion

2 cloves of garlic

½ tbsp fresh rosemary

olive oil

salt and black pepper

200g tempeh

1 heaped tsp white miso paste

1 tsp dried oregano

1 tbsp nutritional yeast

1 tbsp tomato purée

2 tbsp oats

2 tbsp breadcrumbs

1 batch Nonna's pasta sauce (see page 124)

pasta or polenta of your choice, to serve

TIP ◆
These actually taste even better the next day, just heat them up in some of Nonna's Sauce!

1. In a small bowl combine the ground flaxseed and 3 tablespoons of cold water. Set aside for 10 minutes to thicken.

2. Finely dice the onion, finely slice the garlic, and finely chop the rosemary. Add a good drizzle of olive oil to a non-stick pan on a medium heat. Add the onions and fry gently for 5–10 minutes, until soft and golden, then add the garlic and rosemary and season with salt and black pepper. Mix well and fry for a further 1–2 minutes, until the garlic is cooked.

3. Put the tempeh, miso paste, cooked onions, flaxseed mixture, dried oregano, half a teaspoon of salt, nutritional yeast, tomato purée, oats and breadcrumbs into a food processor and pulse briefly, just until broken down and combined but the mixture still has texture. Transfer to a large bowl.

4. Taking a walnut-sized amount of mix at a time, roll the mixture into balls. Be quite firm when rolling, as this will help them keep their shape when frying. You should end up with roughly 20 meatballs. If you find the mix sticky to work with, slightly wet your hands. Transfer to the fridge on a large tray or plate for 20 minutes to firm up.

5. Heat the remaining 2 tablespoons of olive oil in a large frying pan and add the meatballs. Fry for 4–5 minutes, until they are nicely caramelized, crunchy and cooked through. Swirl the pan every so often so that they colour evenly all over.

6. Serve with Nonna's tomato sauce (page 124) and some pasta or polenta.

PESTO THREE WAYS

SERVES: *4*

Call me crazy, but I never use store-bought pesto! That's because it's so easy to make your own, and it tastes ten times better. Here we have not one, not two, but three traditional Italian pesto variations, with only very minor tweaks to make them plant-based. The basil pesto is the classic you know and love, the pistachio pesto is a creamier version with a deep, rich, nutty flavour, and the pesto alla Trapanese is a traditional recipe from Trapani, which uses almonds and cherry tomatoes for a lighter, tomatoey pesto! All these are great as dips or as a sauce for your favourite pasta – just remember to mix them with a good amount of pasta cooking water to make them silky-smooth.

Basil Pesto

PREP TIME: *20 mins*

INGREDIENTS ♦

60g pine nuts (or raw cashews for a cheaper option)

100g fresh basil

1 small clove of garlic

30g vegan Parmesan (or cashew Parmesan, page 28)

juice of ½ a lemon

salt and pepper

175ml extra virgin olive oil

To serve (optional)

300g pasta of your choice

1. Toast the pine nuts in a dry pan on a medium heat until they are golden brown.

2. Pick the basil leaves. If using a blender, simply pulse all the remaining ingredients, except the pine nuts and olive oil, until a smooth texture is achieved. This method is much easier but not as authentic! Then skip to step 6.

3. If using a pestle and mortar, start by roughly chopping the basil leaves and crushing the garlic. Put the garlic and basil into your mortar and start to grind until well combined.

4. Add the vegan Parmesan, lemon juice, salt and pepper and combine again until a smooth consistency is achieved (some lumps are OK!).

5. Next, add the toasted pine nuts and process until they break down, then very slowly add the oil, 1 tablespoon at a time. The whole process should take about 20 minutes – it's an arm workout!

6. To serve with pasta, cook your pasta, then drain, reserving a mug of cooking water, and transfer to a serving bowl.

7. Add the pesto and mix until it coats the pasta evenly. If necessary, add some of the reserved pasta water.

Pesto Di Pistacchio (Sicilian Pesto)

PREP TIME: *20 mins*

INGREDIENTS ◆

100g raw pistachios

1 small clove of garlic

75g cashew Parmesan (page 28)

75ml extra virgin olive oil

a squeeze of lemon juice

a pinch of salt

To serve (optional)

300g pasta of your choice

1. Lightly toast the pistachios in a dry non-stick pan on a medium heat. Stay with the pan to make sure they don't burn. Once they are lightly toasted, turn off the heat.

2. Crush the garlic and put it into a food processor with the toasted pistachios, cashew Parmesan, oil, lemon juice and salt. Give it a few pulses – you still want to have some lumps of pistachio!

3. To serve with pasta, cook your pasta according to the packet instructions and drain, reserving a few ladles of the pasta cooking water (about 200ml). Transfer to a serving bowl, add the pesto and pasta water, and mix everything together until nice and creamy.

4. Serve with extra cashew Parmesan and a drizzle of olive oil, and enjoy.

Pesto alla Trapanese

PREP TIME: *10 mins*

INGREDIENTS ◆

1 clove of garlic

75g toasted blanched almonds

10 large fresh basil leaves

6 fresh mint leaves

250g vine-ripened cherry tomatoes

1 tbsp vegan Parmesan (or cashew Parmesan, page 28)

70ml extra virgin olive oil

salt and pepper

To serve (optional)

300g pasta of your choice

1. Place all the ingredients in a mortar and crush with the pestle until you have a bright green sauce. Or add all the ingredients to a food processor or blender and pulse briefly until you get a chunky sauce. Season with salt and pepper to taste.

2. To serve with pasta, cook your pasta according to the packet instructions and drain. Transfer to a serving bowl, add the pesto, and mix together.

TIPS ◆

Use a pestle and mortar for the most authentic pesto. If you're in a rush, you can use a high-speed blender, but the texture will have a uniform consistency. A pesto made in a pestle and mortar will combine all the flavours and oils of all the ingredients while maintaining a varied consistency – which is exactly what we want!

Never put the oil in the pestle and mortar first. You always want to grind the other ingredients first to release their natural oils.

Gnocchi is one of those simple dishes that's really easy to make at home, and it's naturally plant-based, when made with flour and potato. This spruced-up version is perfect for a comforting night in, when you fancy something different to regular pasta.

GNOCCHI CON SALVIA E BURRO FUSO

Sage Gnocchi with Almond Brown Butter

SERVES: *4*
PREP TIME: *15 mins*
COOKING TIME: *1 hour 30 mins*

INGREDIENTS ◆

600g large floury potatoes (Maris Piper or King Edward)

olive oil

fine salt

100g Tipo 00 flour or plain flour

50g cornflour

2 tbsp plant-based milk

a pinch of ground turmeric

freshly ground black pepper

vegan Parmesan, to serve

Sauce

100g plant-based butter

3 cloves of garlic

1½ tbsp ground almonds

a small handful of fresh sage leaves

a generous grating of nutmeg

1. Preheat the oven to 190°C fan/210°C. Place the potatoes on a baking tray, prick them a few times with a fork and rub with a little olive oil and salt. Bake in the oven for 1–1½ hours, or until cooked through (this will depend on the size of the potatoes). Remove from the oven and set aside for 5 minutes so they are just cool enough to handle.

2. Cut the potatoes in half and scoop the flesh into a mixing bowl. Add the flour, cornflour, plant-based milk, turmeric, 1 teaspoon of fine salt and some freshly ground black pepper, then use a wooden spoon to combine it into a dough.

3. Tip the dough on to a floured work surface and knead gently for 1 minute. This will help bring the dough together and give it a bit more bite. Don't be tempted to knead for longer or it will go tough.

4. Keeping the surface nicely floured, divide the dough into 4 pieces. Roll each piece into a long sausage shape about the thickness of your thumb (roughly 2cm across), then use a knife to cut the sausage into 2cm pieces.

5. You can either leave the gnocchi like this, or you can make them into the traditional ridged gnocchi shape. If you want to do this, you will need a special gnocchi board or a fork. Place a piece of gnocchi on the board or on the back of the fork. Place your thumb on top and gently press down, rolling it over the board or the tines of the fork. Repeat with the rest of the pieces.

»

6. Oil a baking tray, and bring a large pan of salted water to the boil over a high heat. Once boiling, add the gnocchi and cook for 4–5 minutes, or until the gnocchi have just floated to the surface of the water. Remove with a slotted spoon and place on the oiled tray while you make the sauce.

7. Melt the butter in a large frying pan over a medium heat. Grate in the garlic and stir in the ground almonds. Cook for 2–3 minutes, or until the butter is foamy and the almonds and garlic are just turning golden and caramelized. Add the sage leaves, followed by the cooked gnocchi.

8. Fry the gnocchi for 4–5 minutes, tossing them in the foaming butter until they are nicely coated in the almonds and are starting to crisp on the outside. If the almonds start to colour too much, turn the heat to low.

9. Add a good amount of salt and pepper, and a generous grating of nutmeg.

10. Serve in bowls, with any remaining butter from the pan spooned over the top. Finish with lots of vegan Parmesan.

Pumpkin and hazelnuts are very common ingredients in Italian cuisine, and this is a creamy and decadent pasta dish with a nutty twist. Try to find a small pumpkin with a dark green skin; alternatively, butternut squash works well.

RIGATONI ALLA ZUCCA
Pumpkin & Hazelnut Rigatoni

SERVES: *2*
PREP TIME: *15 mins*
COOKING TIME: *45 mins*

INGREDIENTS ◆

1 medium butternut squash or pumpkin

4 unpeeled cloves of garlic

3 tbsp olive oil

salt and pepper

80g hazelnuts

½ tbsp sliced fresh sage leaves

300ml vegetable stock

150g rigatoni pasta

50ml vegan double cream

whole nutmeg, for grating

Hazelnut and sage pangrattato

30g hazelnuts

1 tbsp olive oil

2 tbsp chopped fresh sage leaves

2 tbsp coarse breadcrumbs

1. Preheat the oven to 190°C fan/210°C.

2. Peel and deseed the squash or pumpkin, then dice into 3cm chunks and place in a roasting tin with the unpeeled garlic. Drizzle with the olive oil and season. Toss to coat everything in oil and seasoning. Roast for 30–35 minutes, stirring occasionally, until cooked through and beginning to caramelize.

3. Meanwhile, put the hazelnuts into a pan with 500ml of water and bring to a simmer. Cook for 15 minutes, until softened, then drain.

4. Transfer two-thirds of the roasted squash to a blender. Squeeze the garlic pulp from the cloves and add to the blender along with the hazelnuts, sage and a good amount of salt and pepper. Pour in 250ml of veg stock and blend until smooth. If it looks too thick, add more stock and blitz again. Transfer to a pan and set aside.

5. Cook the pasta according to the packet instructions and drain, reserving a cup of pasta cooking water.

6. Meanwhile, make the pangrattato. Chop the hazelnuts, put them into a frying pan with the olive oil and sage, and toast over a medium heat until just starting to turn golden. Add the bread-crumbs and keep frying, stirring constantly, until golden. Transfer the pangrattato to a bowl and season with salt and pepper.

7. Once the pasta is cooked, reheat the sauce over a low flame. Stir in the vegan cream and grate in a little fresh nutmeg. Then stir in the drained pasta, adding a splash of pasta cooking water if necessary.

8. Transfer the pasta to two plates, top with the remaining squash, and sprinkle the pangrattato over the top.

When you are in a rush and want a super quick and sweet tomato pasta that still has that authentic Italian taste, make this. It's ready in 15 minutes and works best with spaghetti. Try to get cherry tomatoes on the vine, and only the deep-red ones (not yellow or orange, as they'll change the colour of the sauce).

PASTA E CILIEGINI
Cherry Tomato Pasta

SERVES: *2–3*
PREP TIME: *10 mins*
COOKING TIME: *15 mins*

INGREDIENTS ◆

400g cherry tomatoes

2–3 cloves of garlic

extra virgin olive oil

½ tsp chilli flakes

a pinch of salt

1 tsp sugar

¼ tsp bicarbonate of soda

a handful of fresh basil

200g spaghetti

vegan or cashew Parmesan, to serve

1. Remove the cherry tomatoes from the stems and slice them in half. Thinly slice the garlic.

2. Put 3 tablespoons of olive oil into a deep frying pan and add the sliced garlic. Bring to a medium heat, making sure the garlic doesn't burn.

3. Once the oil is heated and the garlic is bubbling away, add the tomatoes and bring to a simmer.

4. Add the chilli flakes, salt, sugar and bicarbonate of soda, and mix well. Let the acidity bubble out for 30 seconds while stirring. Lightly mash the tomatoes using the back of a wooden spoon, to extract their juices.

5. Tear in some of the fresh basil leaves and mix again. Keep on a low simmer.

6. Cook your spaghetti in salted boiling water according to the packet instructions, then drain, reserving a little of the cooking water.

7. Transfer the cooked pasta to the pan of sauce and mix every-thing together, adding a little pasta cooking water. Serve immediately, with fresh Parmesan and the rest of the basil leaves.

Arguably the ultimate Italian dish: traditionally made with creamy béchamel, lots of cheese and a meat sauce, this plant-based version has everything you'd expect and more. You can use store-bought plant-based mince or my walnut and mushroom ragù on page 162.

LASAGNE

SERVES: 6
PREP TIME: 20 mins
COOKING TIME: 90 mins

INGREDIENTS ◆

1 small carrot

2 stalks of celery

2 banana shallots

4 cloves of garlic

4 tbsp olive oil

460g plant-based mince or homemade ragù (see page 162)

2 x 400g tins of chopped tomatoes

a pinch of chilli flakes

1 tbsp sugar

1½ tsp salt

¼ tsp bicarbonate of soda

1 pack of egg-free lasagne sheets

200g vegan mozzarella, grated

Béchamel

50g plant-based butter

1 spring onion

50g plain flour

500ml oat milk

½ tsp grated nutmeg

salt and black pepper

1. Slice the carrot, celery and shallots and blend with the garlic. Once blended, put the mixture into a saucepan and fry on a medium heat for 10 minutes.

2. Add your plant-based mince of choice and let it brown for 6–8 minutes (you can use green lentils or my walnut and mushroom ragù to keep the dish more wholefood plant-based). Add the tinned tomatoes and one tin's worth of water.

3. Bring to a low simmer, then add the chilli flakes, sugar, salt and bicarbonate of soda. Stir well until all the bubbles have gone from the soda, then slightly reduce the heat and simmer for 20–30 minutes.

4. Next, prepare the béchamel. Melt the plant-based butter in a pan and add the sliced spring onion. Gradually add the flour then whisk continuously while adding the milk until all is combined. Add salt, nutmeg and pepper to taste. Keep stirring until the sauce thickens, then turn off the heat.

5. Preheat the oven to 160°C fan/180°C and grease a baking dish with vegan butter or oil.

6. Start layering: first a dollop of pasta sauce, then a layer of lasagne sheets, then a thin layer of the sauce, a few dollops of béchamel and a sprinkle of cheese. Repeat until everything is used up.

7. Cover with foil and bake in the oven for 30 minutes. Then remove the foil and bake for an additional 10 minutes. The crust on top should be golden brown.

8. Take the dish out of the oven and wait 10 minutes before serving.

NOTE ◆
The best thing about this dish is that it is lighter than traditional lasagne, while still being rich and delicious. It also freezes really well.

This is one of those dishes that instantly brings back memories of being a child and is so comforting yet simple. It's the first thing Nonna makes whenever one of her twenty-two grandchildren or great grandchildren are feeling under the weather. I grew up with Nonna adding a block of Babybel cheese to melt inside this dish and make it all creamy, but with a simple swap to plant-based cream cheese, it tastes just like Nonna's but is completely vegan!

Pastina means little pasta. You don't need to use star shapes – you can use any small pasta, or even thin spaghetti broken up very small – but for me stars are the most traditional.

PASTINA
Little Pasta

SERVES: *2*
PREP TIME: *5 mins*
COOKING TIME: *10 mins*

INGREDIENTS ◆

1 vegetable stock cube

200g stelline
(star-shaped pasta)

40g vegan cream cheese
(Nush or philadelphia
works well)

a little plant-based milk

salt and black pepper

grated vegan Parmesan
(optional)

1. Put 1½ litres of water into a large saucepan with the veg stock cube and bring to the boil.

2. Add the pasta and cook until soft and most of the liquid has been absorbed. If you prefer it to have a little bite, cook until al dente, but if it's for a small child, cook the pasta right through.

3. Turn off the heat and add the cream cheese and a dash of plant-based milk, stirring well so the cheese melts.

4. Serve with a pinch of salt and pepper to taste if needed, and a sprinkling of vegan Parmesan if you like.

TIPS ◆

You can blend some boiled vegetables (carrots, celery, shallots) into the pasta to add more nutrients and texture – great for weaning babies.

If you don't have stelline, you can use thin spaghetti, broken up very small.

When I asked Nonna to help me make a vegan cacio e pepe she laughed in my face – but I was intent on veganizing this classic Italian dish. It's so much simpler than you think, and it uses my homemade cashew Parmesan, which I like to make in bulk and store in the fridge.

CACIO E PEPE
Pasta with Cheese & Black Pepper

SERVES: *3–4*
PREP TIME: *10 mins*
COOKING TIME: *15 mins*

INGREDIENTS ◆

350 dried linguine, bucatini or spaghetti

8 tbsp olive oil, approx. 150ml

1 tsp coarse, freshly ground black pepper

Cashew Parmesan
120g raw cashews

3 tbsp nutritional yeast

½ tsp garlic powder

½ tsp onion powder

½ tsp flaky salt

1. Place all the ingredients for the cashew Parmesan in a small food processor or blender and blitz to a fine powder.

2. Cook the pasta until al dente in a large pan of salted boiling water. When the pasta is cooked, reserve 200ml of the pasta water before draining.

3. Heat the olive oil in a deep frying pan over a medium-low heat. Add the ground pepper. It should sizzle immediately. Give it a stir and quickly add 5 tablespoons of the cashew Parmesan. Stir for 30 seconds to combine, then pour in the reserved pasta water.

4. Raise the heat to medium-high and bring quickly to the boil, stirring all the time. Boil until the sauce has thickened and is rich and creamy. Add the pasta to the sauce and toss until fully coated. Taste and season with salt if needed.

5. Serve in bowls, with the extra cashew Parmesan on the side to sprinkle over.

Lentils are a great source of protein, and this recipe is one that needed zero tweaking – aside from the sub for Parmesan – as it's a naturally plant-based *cucina povera* dish. Nonna would traditionally make this on New Year's Eve for us to eat at midnight, as it's supposed to symbolize good luck for the year ahead. We would wear red on New Year's Eve for the same reason – don't ask me why, we've just always done it and we've been pretty lucky so far!

PASTA CON LENTICCHIE
Pasta with Lentils

SERVES: *4*
PREP TIME: *10 mins*
COOKING TIME: *30 mins*

INGREDIENTS ◆

200g dried green lentils

1 white onion or 2 shallots (approx. 60g)

1 large stalk of celery

1 large carrot

1 veg stock cube

150g pasta (Nonna suggests capellini spezzati or regular angel hair spaghetti, broken up)

extra virgin olive oil

plant-based or cashew Parmesan (see page 28), to serve

1. Place the lentils into a sieve and give them a quick rinse under cold water, then put in a saucepan with 1 litre of water and bring to a simmer with a good pinch of salt.

2. Meanwhile, finely dice all the veg (if you prefer, you can blitz them in a food processor to save on chopping time) and add to the simmering lentils.

3. Crumble in the veg stock cube and simmer everything for about 20 minutes, then add the pasta and cook for a further 6–8 minutes, by which point the pasta should be al dente and the lentils should be nice and soft.

4. Once the lentils and pasta are cooked, season to taste, then transfer them to a large dish. Serve with a good drizzle of olive oil and a sprinkling of Parmesan.

Nonna doesn't like saying the name of this one, as it's a rude word – but she definitely likes eating it! This recipe is super close to the original, just without the anchovies, though as long as you get good-quality olives and capers, you'll hardly notice the difference.

PASTA ALLA PUTTANESCA
Pasta with Olives & Capers

SERVES: *2–3*
PREP TIME: *10 mins*
COOKING TIME: *20 mins*

INGREDIENTS ◆

2–3 cloves of garlic

2 shallots

2 tbsp extra virgin olive oil

salt and black pepper

150g capers, drained

150g pitted Kalamata olives

600ml tomato passata or Nonna's pasta sauce (page 124)

a pinch of chilli flakes

1 tsp sugar

¼–½ tsp bicarbonate of soda

300g dried pasta of your choice

a pinch of dried parsley

plant-based or cashew Parmesan (see page 28)

1. Finely slice or grate the garlic cloves along with the shallots, and fry them in olive oil for 2–3 minutes on a medium heat, until softened.

2. Meanwhile, bring a pan of water to the boil and add 1 tablespoon of fine salt.

3. Once the shallots are translucent, add the capers and olives and stir everything together. (Slice the olives in half lengthways if you don't like them whole.)

4. Add the passata or Nonna's pasta sauce and slightly increase the heat to bring to a simmer, adding a touch of water if needed.

5. Add the chilli flakes, sugar and bicarbonate of soda (not too much!), and stir. Season to taste with salt and slightly reduce the heat, letting it simmer for 5–10 minutes.

6. Cook your pasta until al dente, then drain, reserving a cupful of the cooking water. Add the pasta to the puttanesca sauce.

7. Give everything a good stir and add the ladle or two of pasta cooking water to help the sauce become nice and glossy.

8. Serve with a sprinkle of dried parsley and vegan Parmesan.

Nonna
APPROVED

This hits all the spots of a traditional carbonara: the texture is silky-smooth, we've got salty tempeh 'bacon' bits, and it even has the eggy taste thanks to the black salt – be careful, though, that salt goes a long way, so a tiny sprinkle just before serving is what I recommend!

CARBONARA
Creamy Carbonara with Pangrattato

SERVES: *3–4*
PREP TIME: *15 mins*
COOKING TIME: *20 mins*

INGREDIENTS ◆

300g linguine
½ tbsp chopped sage
50g cashew Parmesan
   (page 28)

Carbonara sauce
80g raw cashews
1 clove of garlic
300g silken tofu
4 tbsp nutritional yeast
1 tsp onion powder
150ml plant milk
¼ tsp ground turmeric
½ tsp Dijon mustard
50ml extra virgin olive oil
black salt & pepper

Tempeh 'bacon'
2 tbsp olive oil
200g tempeh
1½ tbsp light soy sauce
1 tbsp agave syrup
½ tsp smoked paprika

Pangrattato
2 cloves of garlic, crushed
50g walnuts, chopped
100g sourdough or
   ciabatta
1 tbsp olive oil
1 tbsp chopped sage

1. To make the carbonara sauce, boil the cashews and garlic clove in a pan of water for 10 minutes, then drain. This helps reduce the bitter taste.

2. Put the boiled cashews and garlic into a blender with the silken tofu, nutritional yeast, onion powder, plant milk, turmeric, Dijon mustard, olive oil and a pinch of black salt and pepper. Blend until smooth, then set aside.

3. For the tempeh 'bacon' add 2 tablespoons of olive oil to a pan over a medium heat. Dice the tempeh into 1–2 cm cubes and add to the pan. Fry until they start to brown, then add the soy sauce, agave syrup and smoked paprika and fry until golden brown. Remove from the pan and set aside.

4. To make the pangrattato, put the sourdough into a food processor and pulse to chunky breadcrumbs. Heat the olive oil in a frying pan over a medium heat and add the garlic. Stir briefly, then add the breadcrumbs. Fry until lightly golden, then add the sage, salt, pepper and walnuts. Fry for a few minutes until the walnuts are toasted and the bread is golden. Set aside.

5. Cook your pasta for 1–2 minutes less than the packet instructions (al dente) and drain, reserving 2–3 ladles of cooking water.

6. Put the carbonara mixture into a saucepan, and add the cooked pasta and reserved pasta water. Mix well and season with salt if needed, and lots of freshly ground black pepper. Stir in the fresh sage and half the tempeh bacon.

7. Serve immediately, topped with the remaining tempeh bacon, a pinch of black salt and the pangrattato.

Walnuts and sunflower seeds are not only nutritional power-houses packed with healthy omega-3s, but they also make a great wholefood mince alternative. This rich sauce is super versatile and works great in lasagne, but serving it with pappardelle is my favourite way to enjoy it.

BOLOGNESE DI NOCI E FUNGHI
Walnut & Mushroom Ragu

SERVES: *4*
PREP TIME: *20 mins*
COOKING TIME: *40 mins*

INGREDIENTS ◆

120g walnuts

80g sunflower seeds

2 stalks of celery

1 small carrot

1 white onion or
2 shallots

4 tbsp extra virgin
olive oil

3 cloves of garlic

250g chestnut
mushrooms

salt and black pepper

2 tbsp tomato purée

2 x 400g tins of chopped
tomatoes

400g tomato passata

1 tsp white miso paste

½ tsp chilli flakes

1 tsp dried oregano

¼ tsp bicarbonate of
soda

a bunch of fresh basil
(20g)

1 tsp sugar

300g pappardelle or
other pasta of choice

grated vegan Parmesan

1. Put the walnuts and sunflower seeds into a small bowl, cover with hot water and set aside for 20 minutes.

2. Wash the celery and chop the ends off, peel the carrot and onion, and put them all into a food processor (roughly chop if they won't fit). Blitz until they are broken down into small chunks. Heat 2 tablespoons of olive oil in a large pan over a medium heat, then add the blitzed veg and the crushed garlic. Cook for 5 minutes.

3. Remove the stems from the mushrooms, then put them into the food processor and pulse a few times until they break into mince-sized chunks. (Divide the mushrooms into two batches if needed.)

4. Add the mushroom chunks to the pan, season with a good pinch of salt and pepper, and cook for a further 5–10 minutes, until the mushrooms have softened, stirring occasionally.

5. Meanwhile, drain the walnuts and sunflower seeds and put them into the food processor. Blend for 20–30 seconds, until they become almost a paste, but with some small chunks left. Add the nutty paste to the pan along with the tomato purée. Mix everything together to combine.

6. Add the tinned tomatoes, passata, miso paste, chilli flakes, oregano, bicarbonate of soda, sugar and the bunch of fresh basil. Adjust the heat to a low simmer, stir for 30 seconds while bubbling, season to taste, and leave for 20 minutes. (Pop on a lid if you have one!).

7. Meanwhile, cook your pasta of choice in salted boiling water until al dente, then drain and place in a large serving bowl. Add a quarter of the ragù and stir to coat the pasta then serve with an extra helping of the ragù, and top with a drizzle of olive oil and a sprinkling of vegan Parmesan.

Nonna
APPROVED

Pasta with broccoli is Nonna's all-time favourite pasta dish – but she doesn't get to make it as often as she likes because Nonno only likes to eat pasta with tomato sauce every single day! This is one of my most viral dishes on social media and so many people tell me they make it at least once a week.

PASTA CON I BROCCOLI
Pasta with Broccoli

SERVES: *2–3*
PREP TIME: *10 mins*
COOKING TIME: *10 mins*

INGREDIENTS ◆

1 large head of broccoli

2 cloves of garlic

½ a leek

2 spring onions

2 tbsp extra virgin olive oil

200g pasta of your choice (farfalle, penne, orecchiette)

1 veg stock cube

salt and pepper

1 tbsp toasted breadcrumbs, plus extra for serving

vegan Parmesan (optional)

salt and pepper

1. Bring a saucepan of water to the boil and add 1 tablespoon of salt.

2. Break or slice the broccoli into small chunks, keeping the stalks in too, and boil for 5–6 minutes.

3. While the broccoli is cooking, finely slice the garlic, leek and spring onions. Fry in olive oil on a medium heat until soft (approx. 5–10 minutes).

4. Remove the cooked broccoli from the pan with a slotted spoon and place on a chopping board. Don't throw away the water! Chop the broccoli into smaller chunks and add to the pan of leeks.

5. Add your pasta to the same pan of water you cooked the broccoli in, and cook until al dente. Nonna's favourite shape for this dish is farfalle or 'butterfly', but penne or orecchiette also work well.

6. Season the broccoli mixture with salt and pepper. Dissolve the stock cube in a ladle of the pasta cooking water (approx. 100ml) and add to the vegetables.

7. When the pasta is al dente, transfer it to the vegetable pan, add the breadcrumbs and mix everything together. Add another ladle of pasta water here if needed, to help loosen the mixture.

8. Turn off the heat and serve immediately, with grated Parmesan if you like, and extra toasted breadcrumbs.

This is one of my favourite recipes in the book. Believe it or not, we actually have cannelloni as a starter on Christmas Day, before the main roast dinner. The creamy cashew and spinach ricotta goes perfectly with Nonna's pasta sauce.

CANNELLONI

SERVES: *2–3*
PREP TIME: *30 mins*
COOKING TIME: *40 mins*

INGREDIENTS ◆

1 x Nonna's tomato sauce (page 124)

500g spinach

70g grated vegan cheese

20 cannelloni tubes

Tofu ricotta

100g cashews

1 x 300g block of medium-firm tofu

juice of ½ a lemon

1 tbsp nutritional yeast

2 tbsp plant-based cream cheese or crème fraîche

½ a clove of garlic

1 tsp fine salt

a pinch of black pepper

¼ tsp nutmeg

50ml soy milk

Béchamel

1 spring onion

25g plant-based butter

30g plain flour

250ml oat or soy milk

salt and black pepper

¼ tsp grated nutmeg

1. Start by making a batch of Nonna's tomato sauce (see page 124), and once it's simmering, begin the next step.

2. Place the cashews and garlic clove in a small bowl, cover with hot water and set aside to soak for 30 minutes. Slice the spring onion for the béchamel and set aside.

3. Drain any liquid from the tofu and put it into a food processor along with the lemon juice, nutritional yeast, cream cheese, garlic, salt, pepper, nutmeg, soy milk and the drained cashews. Blitz to a smooth paste. Taste and season if needed.

4. Put the spinach into a large pan and add a glass of water. Place it over a high heat, then pop the lid on and let it wilt. (Alternatively, you can use frozen spinach, defrosted and well drained.) Drain the spinach and squeeze out as much water as possible.

5. Roughly chop the drained spinach on a board, then put it into a bowl with the tofu ricotta. Mix well until combined. Season to taste.

6. Now make the béchamel. Melt the butter in a pan and add the sliced spring onion. Gradually add the flour to form a paste, mixing continuously to avoid any lumps.

7. Slowly add the milk, then add salt, pepper and nutmeg to taste. Keep stirring until the sauce thickens, then turn off the heat. (If it's too liquid, sieve in an extra pinch of flour.)

8. Preheat the oven to 180°C fan/200°C.

9. To assemble the cannelloni, place the spinach ricotta mix in a plastic freezer bag or piping bag, and snip off the end.

»

10. Evenly spread a few dollops of tomato sauce over the base of a 30 x 20cm ovenproof baking dish.

11. Fill the cannelloni tubes with the ricotta mix and lay them in the dish, repeating until the dish is filled with the stuffed tubes.

12. Generously cover with Nonna's tomato sauce, making sure you can't see any of the cannelloni.

13. Dollop the béchamel over the tomato sauce, then lightly swirl it with a spoon to mix it with the sauce.

14. Top with the grated vegan cheese, then wrap the baking dish in foil and bake in the oven for 30 minutes. Then remove the foil and bake for a further 10 minutes at 200°C.

This is my take on the Italian pasta dish 'alla norcina'. Typically made using sausage and cream, it uses a store-bought plant-based sausage, homemade cashew cream and white wine to give a rich depth to the sauce, plus fennel seeds to give a little kick.

PASTA CREMOSA CON CAVOLO E SALSICCIA

Creamy Sausage & Cavolo Nero Pasta

SERVES: *2*
PREP TIME: *15 mins*
COOKING TIME: *15 mins*

INGREDIENTS ◆

85g raw cashews

100g cavolo nero

2 shallots

2 cloves of garlic

200g dried pasta

2 tbsp extra virgin olive oil, plus extra for drizzling and finishing

150g vegan sausages (4 Richmond or THIS sausages)

½ tbsp finely chopped fresh rosemary

½ tsp crushed fennel seeds

50ml white wine

100ml soy milk

150ml vegetable stock

salt and black pepper

2 tbsp cashew Parmesan (page 28), plus extra for serving (optional)

1. Place the cashews in a small bowl, cover with boiling water and set aside for 15 minutes.

2. Remove the stems from the cavolo nero. Finely slice the shallots and grate the garlic.

3. Cook the pasta in a pan of salted boiling water until al dente. For the final minute, add the cavolo nero to the pan. Reserve a few ladles of pasta water, then drain the pasta and cavolo nero, put back into the pan, toss through a drizzle of olive oil and set aside.

4. While the pasta is cooking, put 2 tablespoons of extra virgin olive oil into a large frying pan on a medium heat and add the shallots and garlic. Cook for 5 minutes, until the shallots have softened.

5. Remove the skins from the sausages and break them into small chunks, then add them to the pan and fry until golden.

6. Add the rosemary and fennel seeds and fry for 30 seconds, then add the wine and let it reduce until most of the liquid is gone.

7. While the wine is reducing, put the drained cashews, soy milk and veg stock into a blender and blitz until smooth.

8. Add the cashew mix to the sausage pan and season well. Stir in some of the pasta water to achieve a silky-smooth consistency.

9. Add the cooked pasta and cavolo nero and mix well. Season to taste and stir in the cashew Parmesan, if using.

10. Spoon into bowls and finish with more cashew Parmesan, a drizzle of olive oil and plenty of freshly ground black pepper.

TIP ◆

In this recipe, and in any other pasta
recipe using a cashew cream sauce,
pasta cooking water is your best friend
– the sauce can thicken up really
quickly, depending on the heat and
how long you leave it before eating,
so always keep some extra on hand
to loosen up the sauce if needed.

Nothing says classic Italian pasta night better than Nonna's pasta al forno! I've fed this to friends on several occasions and they can't get enough. It's kind of like a lasagne but with fewer steps, and it uses any pasta shape you like, though the most traditional is rigatoni.

PASTA AL FORNO
Baked Pasta

SERVES: *3*
PREP TIME: *20 mins*
COOKING TIME: *1 hour*

INGREDIENTS ◆

250g pasta (rigatoni is best)

150g frozen peas

100g plant-based mozzarella

40g grated plant-based Parmesan

3 tbsp plant-based single cream

60g breadcrumbs

Nonna's pasta sauce

2 shallots or 1 white onion

1 medium carrot

2 cloves of garlic

1 stalk of celery

2 tbsp olive oil

220g plant-based mince

2 x 400g tins of chopped tomatoes

1 tbsp salt

¼ tsp chilli flakes

1 tbsp sugar

20g fresh or frozen basil

¼ tsp bicarbonate of soda

1. Preheat the oven to 180°C fan/200°C. Blend the onion, carrot, garlic and celery in a food processor and fry in 2 tablespoons of olive oil on a medium heat for 5 minutes.

2. Add the mince and brown for 5 minutes, making sure to break it up into small chunks if needed.

3. Blend the tomatoes in the food processor or with a hand blender and add to the pan, along with 1–2 tins' worth of water. Bring to the boil.

4. Add the salt, chilli flakes, sugar, basil and bicarbonate of soda. Let the acid bubble out, then reduce the heat and let the sauce simmer for 20 minutes minimum, adding the frozen peas in the last 3 minutes.

5. Meanwhile, bring a pot of salted water to the boil and cook your pasta for 3 minutes less than the packet instructions – you want it to be cooked through but still with a bit of a bite (al dente). While it's cooking, mix in 2 tablespoons of olive oil to prevent sticking.

6. Drain the pasta, then put it back into the empty saucepan. Add a ladle or two of the mince and give it a good stir.

7. Transfer the pasta to a baking tray and top with most of the sauce. Add a sprinkling of cheese, the plant-based cream and breadcrumbs, and finish with a few more dollops of sauce. Bake in the oven for 20–25 minutes or until it's golden and bubbling on top.

TIPS ◆

It's always best to cook your pasta al dente because it's going to be cooked again in the oven!

This dish ALWAYS tastes better the next day, or at least once it's been sitting for a while, so it's a great dish to make ahead of a dinner party. Make it the night before, then simply reheat it in the oven to serve.

SECONDI PIATTI

Main Courses

Nonna
APPROVED

This one's a classic that Nonna loves to cook as it was one of the most popular dishes in the restaurant. The tomato sauce is the exact same as the pasta sauce we make. To replace the chicken, we use firm tofu, but you could equally use a store-bought plant-based chicken. You can also serve this dish with pasta, but Nonna likes to serve it as an antipasto with bread or crackers.

TOFU ALLA CACCIATORE
Tofu Cacciatore

SERVES: *4*
PREP TIME: *10 mins*
COOKING TIME: *30 mins*

INGREDIENTS ◆

350g plant-based chicken alternative or 400g firm tofu

3 tbsp olive oil

2 mixed peppers

1 white or red onion

200g chestnut mushrooms

2 cloves of garlic

1 glass red wine (150ml)

2 sprigs of fresh thyme

2 tsp dried oregano

½ tsp chilli flakes

1 batch Nonna's pasta sauce (see page 124)

Optionally add 300g pasta of your choice, if serving with pasta

fresh parsley, to serve

vegan Parmesan, to serve

1. Preheat your oven to 180°C fan/200°C (if using, otherwise use an air fryer). Remove your tofu from the pack and drain any excess liquid. Break apart the tofu into rough 3cm chunks, place on a lined baking tray and coat with olive oil, salt, pepper and half the oregano. Give them a quick massage and bake for 20 minutes or air fry for 12.

2. Meanwhile, chop the peppers, onion and mushrooms into small chunks. Crush the garlic.

3. Add the peppers and onion to a pan and fry for 5 minutes.

4. Add the mushrooms and crushed garlic, and continue to fry for 5 minutes until the veg softens.

5. Add the glass of red wine and stir, then simmer for 3 minutes until reduced to cook off the alcohol.

6. Add the cooked tofu (or plant-based chicken if using) and simmer for a further 5 minutes so it cooks more and absorbs the flavour.

7. Meanwhile, if you're serving with pasta, cook it now in salted water until al dente!

8. Add Nonna's pasta sauce, the thyme, oregano and chilli flakes, and cook for a further 5 minutes.

9. Season to taste and serve with fresh parsley and vegan Parmesan.

In my opinion the aubergine (or eggplant) is one of the most underrated vegetables. There's something special about it that allows it to absorb flavour unlike any other vegetable, and it also has the creamiest, almost meaty texture when cooked correctly. This parmigiana is bursting with flavour, and is perfect when you fancy something cheesy and comforting that's a little lighter than a lasagna.

MELANZANE ALLA PARMIGIANA
Aubergine Parmesan

SERVES: *4*
PREP TIME: *15 mins*
COOKING TIME: *60 mins*

INGREDIENTS ◆

3 large aubergines (approx. 1kg)

100–150ml vegetable oil, for frying (sunflower)

5 tbsp extra virgin olive oil

salt

1 tsp dried oregano

180g fresh breadcrumbs

1 batch Nonna's tomato sauce (page 124)

200g grated vegan cheese

50g grated vegan Parmesan

fresh basil leaves, to serve

1. Preheat your oven to 180°C fan/200°C.

2. Cut the top and bottom ends off the aubergines, and peel off the skin.

3. Slice the aubergines lengthways into 1cm-thick pieces (you might find it easier to use a mandolin on a thick setting). Put them into a bowl of heavily salted water (2–3 tablespoons) and leave them to sit for 5–10 minutes.

4. Meanwhile, prepare your frying station. Set a large non-stick pan on the hob and bring to a medium heat. Line a large plate or baking tray with a few sheets of kitchen paper.

5. Once the aubergines have soaked, drain them, shake them dry and pat with kitchen paper. Heat a generous glug of vegetable oil in the pan, then shallow fry the aubergine slices in batches until golden brown on each side. Each slice should take about 2 minutes each side. If the pan looks dry once you turn them over, add another drizzle of oil. Make sure there is always some oil in the pan, otherwise the aubergines will burn! Once a slice is cooked through, place it on the plate lined with kitchen paper and repeat.

6. Once all the aubergine slices are cooked, reduce the heat and remove any remaining vegetable oil with kitchen paper, and add 2 tablespoons of olive oil. Bring to a medium heat and add

»

1 teaspoon of salt and 1 teaspoon of dried oregano. Mix these into the oil, then add the breadcrumbs and fry until toasted and golden brown, swirling the pan occasionally.

7. Now get a baking dish and start layering your parmigiana. The first layer will be a small amount of tomato sauce, then add a layer of aubergines and a sprinkling of breadcrumbs followed by a layer of tomato sauce and a sprinkling of vegan cheese. Repeat until you have 4 layers or your baking dish is full, finishing with the cheese. Drizzle over the remaining 3 tablespoons of extra virgin olive oil (this will help the cheese to melt).

8. Bake your parmigiana for 20–30 minutes, or until the top is crisp and golden and the tomato sauce is bubbling.

9. Leave to rest for 10 minutes, then serve with a sprinkling of fresh basil leaves.

Risotto needs no introduction – it's a classic creamy rice dish bursting with flavour, and a mushroom version like this was popular in Nonna's restaurant. With just a few simple tweaks to make it plant-based, this still packs tonnes of flavour and tastes exactly like how Nonna used to make it.

RISOTTO AI FUNGHI
Mushroom Risotto

SERVES: *3–4*
PREP TIME: *10 mins*
COOKING TIME: *25 mins*

INGREDIENTS ◆

- 15g dried porcini mushrooms
- 1 white onion
- 3 tbsp extra virgin olive oil
- 300g chestnut mushrooms
- 300g arborio rice
- 125ml white wine
- 900ml veg stock (made with 2 veg stock cubes)
- 150g asparagus tips
- salt and freshly ground black pepper
- 125g frozen peas
- 30g vegan butter
- 25g grated vegan Parmesan, plus more to serve
- 1 tbsp chopped fresh parsley, to serve

1. Soak the porcini mushrooms in 200ml of boiling water for 15 minutes.

2. Finely dice the onion and fry in the olive oil on a medium heat for 5 minutes. Slice the chestnut mushrooms and add to the pan. Fry for a further 5 minutes, until the mushrooms are golden.

3. Drain and chop the soaked porcini mushrooms, saving the soaking liquid. Add the soaked mushrooms to the pan and fry for a further minute.

4. Add the rice and stir for 2 minutes. Then add the white wine to deglaze the pan, letting it bubble until it is nearly all absorbed.

5. Add the mushroom soaking liquid and stir until absorbed.

6. Now begin adding the veg stock a ladle at a time, while stirring, and only adding more once the last lot has been absorbed. This process will take about 15–20 minutes, so be patient!

7. When you have one ladle of stock left and the rice is nearly cooked, stir through the asparagus tips and add the final ladle of stock.

8. Once the rice is soft, season with salt and pepper and add the frozen peas.

9. Turn off the heat and stir through the vegan butter and vegan Parmesan until the butter has melted and the risotto is creamy.

10. Scatter over the parsley and serve with more vegan Parmesan and olive oil.

I grew up on Nonna's breadcrumb fried chicken and it's the one thing I'd probably miss the most if it weren't for this incredible recipe. You might be sceptical of tofu replacing chicken, but freezing and defrosting changes the texture completely – it's a labour of love but absolutely worth it!

You can use store-bought panko or fine breadcrumbs, but my favourite (and the way Nonna does it) is to use stale bread-crumbs and a pinch of salt.

COTOLETTA DI TOFU
Breadcrumb Tofu

SERVES: 2
PREP TIME: overnight
COOKING TIME: 20 mins

INGREDIENTS ◆

1 x 400g pack of medium-firm tofu (not super-firm; Cauldron works well)

1 tsp onion powder

1 tsp garlic powder

salt and pepper

50g plain flour

100ml plant-based milk

100g fine breadcrumbs

1 tsp dried oregano

100ml vegetable oil, for frying

1 lemon

1. Carefully remove the tofu from the pack, drain any excess water and pat dry with kitchen paper. Be careful not to break the tofu. You can leave it shaped as it is or cut it into the chicken cutlet shape as shown.

2. Place the tofu in a plastic container and freeze overnight.

3. The next day, remove from the freezer and let the tofu fully defrost.

4. Using kitchen paper, remove as much liquid from the defrosted tofu as possible (the tofu will be quite delicate at this point, so be gentle). Carefully slice the tofu in half down the middle to make thinner slices that resemble a chicken cutlet. Then carefully slice each block horizontally in 3, to make 6 thin slices of tofu.

5. In a small bowl mix together the onion powder and garlic powder and season with salt and pepper.

6. Lay the tofu on a plate or chopping board and lightly season all sides with the onion and garlic mix. If you have time, leave the tofu for 15–20 minutes to marinate.

7. Set up three shallow bowls or plates: one with the flour, one with the plant-based milk, and one with the breadcrumbs.

8. Season the breadcrumbs and milk with salt and pepper, and stir the oregano into the breadcrumbs.

»

9. Working quickly while also being gentle, take a piece of tofu and coat it in the flour, shaking off any excess. Then dip it in the milk, then finally in the breadcrumbs, really pressing in the bread-crumbs so the tofu is completely coated. Set the breadcrumbed tofu on a plate and repeat with the remaining slices.

10. Once the tofu is all coated, put a large non-stick frying pan on a medium heat and add the vegetable oil. Once the oil is hot, place the tofu pieces carefully in the pan and fry until golden brown and crispy on both sides. This should take about 2–3 minutes each side.

11. Once cooked, remove the tofu cutlets to a plate lined with kitchen paper to let excess oil drain.

12. Serve, with Nonna's tomato sauce (page 124), a good squeeze of lemon juice, a scattering of vegan cheese and a big bowl of salad. Or, if you prefer, put them inside a ciabatta, topped with melted cheese and tomato sauce, for the ultimate sandwich!

Unlike most of the recipes in this book, polenta is actually more common in the north of Italy – where my Dad's side of the family is from. My Dad's parents pretty much grew up on polenta and mushrooms foraged from the nearby mountains, so this dish is an ode to my north Italian heritage. It's a rich mushroom and butter bean sauce that tastes almost like a meaty stew, served on a bed of creamy polenta. Delicious.

POLENTA CON FUNGHI E FAGIOLI

Mushroom Ragu with Creamy Polenta & Butter Beans

SERVES: 4
PREP TIME: 10 mins
COOKING TIME: 20 mins

INGREDIENTS ◆

Mushroom ragù

10g dried mixed mushrooms or porcini

2 banana shallots

3 tbsp olive oil plus extra for drizzling

2 portobello mushrooms

150g oyster mushrooms

2 cloves of garlic

1 tbsp tomato purée

a splash of Marsala wine (optional)

250ml vegetable stock

¼ tsp yeast extract

½ tsp red miso paste

salt and pepper

200g butter beans, drained

½ tbsp finely chopped fresh rosemary

3 tbsp chopped fresh parsley, to serve

vegan Parmesan, to serve

1. Soak the dried mushrooms in 150ml of boiling water for 10 minutes, until soft.

2. Finely chop the shallots. Heat 3 tablespoons of oil in a pan, add the shallots, and fry them for roughly 5 minutes, until they have softened.

3. Cut the portobello mushrooms in half across the cap and then into 1cm-thick slices. Using your fingers, pull any large oyster mushrooms apart to make bite-size pieces. Add all the mushrooms to the pan of shallots, then turn up the heat and fry for 3–4 minutes, stirring occasionally, or until the mushrooms are golden.

4. Grate the garlic and add to the pan with the tomato purée and the drained soaked mushrooms (making sure you reserve the soaking liquid). Fry for 2 more minutes.

5. Pour in a splash of Marsala and stir for 30 seconds to deglaze the pan, then add the vegetable stock, mushroom soaking water, yeast extract and miso paste and season with lots of pepper and a little salt.

6. Simmer for 5 minutes. Add the drained beans to the pan along with the rosemary and keep simmering for a further 5 minutes, or until the sauce thickens nicely.

Creamy polenta

200g instant polenta

3 tbsp vegan cream cheese

50g grated vegan Parmesan

1½ tbsp extra virgin olive oil

1 tsp finely chopped fresh rosemary (optional)

TIP ◆

Pour any leftover polenta into Tupperware and store it in the fridge – the next day it will be perfect for frying in a stir-fry or for making crispy polenta cubes.

7. Meanwhile, make the polenta. Bring 1 litre of water to the boil in a large saucepan. Over a medium heat and stirring continuously, shower in the polenta and cook for 5–8 minutes, until the polenta is soft and you have a spoonable, creamy consistency. If it gets too thick, add a splash more water. Stir through the vegan cream cheese, Parmesan, extra virgin olive oil and rosemary, if using.

8. Season to taste, then place a few spoons of polenta on a flat plate and spread out into a circle. Spoon on the mushroom sauce and top with fresh parsley, grated Parmesan and a drizzle of olive oil.

Every bite of this takes me to Italy, and I promise you won't notice there's no meat or dairy in this fully loaded sandwich. We've got a creamy artichoke base, soft Mediterranean grilled vegetables and a punchy basil pesto. Served on a warm ciabatta roll, simply delicious.

PANINI CON MELANZANE, PESTO E POMODORI

Italian Grilled Veg Panini

SERVES: *2*
PREP TIME: *20 mins*
COOKING TIME: *20 mins*

INGREDIENTS ◆

2 aubergines

vegetable oil, for frying

2 ciabatta or panini rolls

4–6 sun-dried tomatoes

a handful of rocket

vegan cream cheese

Pesto

100g fresh basil

2 cloves of garlic

6 tbsp extra virgin olive oil

60g toasted pine nuts (or raw cashews)

30g vegan Parmesan (or cashew Parmesan, page 28)

juice of ½ a lemon

Artichoke dip

a handful of fresh parsley

100g carciofi sott'olio (store-bought or see page 32)

½ a clove of garlic

4 tbsp extra virgin olive oil

a pinch of salt and pepper

juice of ¼ of a lemon

1. Blitz all the pesto ingredients in a food processor until everything is combined (but not smooth, you want some lumps). Season with salt and pepper and set aside.

2. Pick the parsley leaves and blend with the rest of the dip ingredients in a food processor. Set aside.

3. Slice the top and bottom off the aubergines, then, using a mandolin set to approx. 5mm, carefully slice them lengthways. Alternatively slice them by hand using a sharp knife. (If you don't like the skin, you can peel them, but I don't mind it.)

4. Put the aubergine slices into a large bowl of cold water mixed with 1 tablespoon of salt, and set aside for 5–10 minutes.

5. Heat some vegetable oil to a medium-high heat in a large non-stick frying pan. Carefully pour away the water from the bowl and give the aubergine slices a light pat dry.

6. Fry the aubergine slices in batches for about 2 minutes each side, until golden brown on both sides. Once ready, place them on a plate lined with kitchen paper. Roughly chop the sun-dried tomatoes.

7. Halve your ciabatta or panini rolls and toast on the cut side (you can use the pan you fried the aubergines in). Now start building your sandwich, beginning with a layer of the artichoke dip, then a sprinkle of rocket, the sliced aubergine, sun-dried tomatoes, cream cheese and finally dollops of pesto. Put the other half of the roll on top, and serve.

Fennel is arguably one of the most underrated vegetables, because although it has a bitter taste when eaten raw, it becomes deliciously sweet when roasted. Paired with this creamy dip and topped with a punchy gremolata (a traditional Italian accompaniment to meat dishes), this makes the perfect midweek dinner or side dish!

FINOCCHI ARROSTO CON FAGIOLI BIANCHI

Roasted Fennel on White Beans

SERVES: *2*
PREP TIME: *10 mins*
COOKING TIME: *30 mins*

INGREDIENTS ◆

2 large fennel bulbs
extra virgin olive oil
2 cloves of garlic
salt and pepper

White bean dip
300g white beans (cannellini)
1 clove of garlic
50g tahini
juice of 1 lemon
50ml extra virgin olive oil
3–4 ice cubes
sea salt and black pepper

Gremolata
1 small clove of garlic
15g fresh flat-leaf parsley
35g toasted whole almonds
zest of 1 large lemon
juice of ¼ of a lemon
2 tbsp extra virgin olive oil, plus extra for drizzling

1. Preheat the oven to 180°C fan/200°C and line a large baking tray.

2. Remove the outer layer of the fennel bulbs, then slice them into quarters and place on the lined baking tray.

3. Put 3 tablespoons of oil into a small bowl or jar and grate or crush in 2 cloves of garlic. Mix well, then pour over the fennel quarters and give them a good massage to get the oil evenly spread over them.

4. Sprinkle with salt and pepper, and roast for 20–30 minutes until nice and charred, turning halfway through.

5. While the fennel is roasting, make the white bean dip by blending all the ingredients in a food processor or blender until silky-smooth.

6. Grate the garlic for the gremolata, chop the parsley and roughly chop the almonds. Combine all the gremolata ingredients in a bowl and season with salt and black pepper.

7. Spread the white bean dip on a large plate and top with the roasted fennel. Scatter over the gremolata and finish with a good drizzle of extra virgin olive oil and some sea salt flakes.

In case you aren't familiar with cooking artichokes, they have a bit inside called the 'choke', which you must not eat. Nonna cooks this dish without removing the choke and just carefully eats around it, but I'd highly recommend you remove it before cooking, although it can be quite fiddly.

CARCIOFI RIPIENI
Stuffed Artichokes

MAKES: *6*
PREP TIME: *15 mins*
COOKING TIME: *20 mins*

INGREDIENTS ◆

6 ripe artichokes

3 banana shallots

300g toasted fine breadcrumbs

2 tsp fine salt

a pinch of black pepper

2 tbsp cashew Parmesan (page 28) or vegan Parmesan

3 tsp dried parsley

125ml extra virgin olive oil

TIP ◆

If you want to remove the choke, get your hands in there and start removing the innermost petals until you see the fluffy fibrous choke. Carefully scoop this out with a teaspoon, then rinse any remaining bits out under the tap. Place the artichoke in a large bowl filled with water and a squeeze of lemon and repeat with the remaining artichokes.

1. Chop off the stems of the artichokes (save for later) and tear off the dark leaves closest to the stems (these should be quite dry). Rinse the artichokes under the tap, then carefully bash the top of the artichokes on a work surface to loosen up the leaves and help open up the centre.

2. For the breadcrumb filling, finely dice the shallots and put them into a bowl with the breadcrumbs, cashew or vegan Parmesan, salt and pepper, dried parsley and extra virgin olive oil. Mix well so it's all combined.

3. Using a teaspoon, stuff the artichokes with the breadcrumbs. To do this, carefully spread open the leaves and then, using a small spoon and your fingers, push the breadcrumbs into the centre of each one and into as many of the petals as you can.

4. Pack all the artichokes tightly into a saucepan, standing next to each other and facing upwards (so you can see the breadcrumbs).

5. Now carefully fill the saucepan with water to come just over half-way up the artichokes, and add 1 tablespoon of salt to the water.

6. Grab the stems saved from earlier and place them standing up in the saucepan, in any gaps you can find between the artichokes.

7. Bring the water to the boil, then pop on the lid and simmer for 15–20 minutes, or until you can easily remove the leaves from the artichokes.

8. Enjoy these by peeling off the outer leaves and scraping the 'meat' off with your teeth. (Do not eat the actual leaf.) Eat the breadcrumbs and heart with a spoon or a fork, or enjoy on pasta!

When we went to Sicily to shoot some of the photos for this book, we asked each of Nonna's four sisters to bring a dish they like to make that just so happens to be plant-based, and Zia Isabella made these delicious roast potatoes. They're the perfect side to a salad for a light lunch, or they can be paired with grilled vegetables and pizza for a comforting dinner.

ZIA ISABELLA'S PATATE AL FORNO
Roast Potato & Veg Gratin

SERVES: *2*
PREP TIME: *10 mins*
COOKING TIME: *30 mins*

INGREDIENTS ◆

300g Maris Piper potatoes

a pinch of salt and pepper

a pinch of dried oregano

extra virgin olive oil

1 large white onion, sliced

150g cherry vine tomatoes

2 red bell peppers, sliced into thin strips

1. Preheat the oven to 180°C fan/200°C.

2. Peel and cut the potatoes into approximately 6cm cubes.

3. Place them in a large bowl and add the salt and pepper, oregano and a good drizzle of extra virgin olive oil, then give them a good toss so they're all coated.

4. Put the onion, cherry tomatoes and red peppers on a large, oiled baking tray, then add the potatoes and give everything a small shake so it's all sitting flat on the tray.

5. Bake in the oven for 30 minutes. Halfway through the cooking time, give the vegetables a stir.

6. Serve immediately.

If you don't like spinach, I can confidently say this recipe will have you questioning yourself! It's made with a few simple ingredients and completely elevates the bland taste of raw spinach. It's traditionally served with meat, but it would also be great as a side to Nonna's polpette or lasagne, or served with a salad for a light lunch. Nonna likes to roughly chop the spinach so it's easier for her to eat, but I prefer to keep it whole!

SPINACI SALTATI CON OLIVE E CAPPERI

Sautéed Spinach with Olives & Capers

SERVES: *2*
PREP TIME: *5 mins*
COOKING TIME: *5 mins*

INGREDIENTS ◆

500g baby spinach, washed

2 cloves of garlic

50g pitted black olives

2 tbsp olive oil plus extra for drizzling

1 tbsp capers

juice of ½ a lemon

1 tbsp plant-based or cashew Parmesan (see page 28)

a pinch of salt and black pepper

1. Bring a large pan of water to the boil and add the spinach. Press it down with a wooden spoon so it's all covered and let it boil for 30–60 seconds. You want to just soften the spinach but not lose the bright green colour.

2. Transfer the spinach to a sieve and run it under cold water to stop it cooking. Then squeeze it with your hands to remove as much water as possible.

3. Thinly slice the garlic and cut the olives in half.

4. Put 2 tablespoons of olive oil into a medium frying pan and add the garlic, olives and capers. Bring to a medium heat and fry for 30–60 seconds, until just golden.

5. Add the spinach to the pan and sauté for 3–5 minutes, until just wilted. Remove from the heat and season with salt and pepper, then stir through the lemon juice and vegan Parmesan.

6. Transfer to a serving dish and drizzle over a little olive oil to serve.

A quick, easy and nutrient-dense dish that works perfectly as meal prep, a side dish to an evening meal or a light summery dinner.

COUSCOUS DI VERDURE MISTE
Mediterranean Couscous

SERVES: *4*
PREP TIME: *10 mins*
COOKING TIME: *30 mins*

INGREDIENTS ◆

1 large courgette (approx. 300g)

1 yellow pepper

1 red pepper

½ a red onion

olive oil

1 clove of garlic

225g butter beans, drained and rinsed

200g couscous

1 veg stock cube

100g pitted black olives

30g fresh basil

extra virgin olive oil

juice of ½ a lemon

TIP ◆

This is a great meal that lasts all week in the fridge and goes really well with a protein such as grilled tofu, air-fried tempeh or edamame beans!

I. Preheat the oven to 160°C fan/180°C.

2. Slice all the veggies into chunks. I like to chop off the top and tail of the courgette, slice it in half lengthways and in half again so there are 4 long batons, then cut the batons into approx. 1cm chunks, almost like small pizza slices. Slice the peppers into 2cm squares – not too tiny. Red onions can be sliced quite small, as they're quite strong.

3. Put all the veggies into a large bowl. Season with salt, pepper and olive oil, then grate over the garlic and give them a good toss so they're all evenly coated. Transfer to a baking tray lined with baking parchment, spreading them out so they all have equal space. Roast in the oven for about 25 minutes, shaking halfway through if you like.

4. 5 minutes before the veg are cooked, add the butter beans to the baking tray and give everything a good shake. Return to the oven for the remaining 5 minutes.

5. Meanwhile, put the couscous into a large, heatproof bowl. Mix the stock cube with 250ml of hot water and pour over the couscous. (You can also use liquid veg stock or powder.) Stir, then set aside.

6. Slice the black olives and finely chop the basil. Once the veg are cooked, add them to the couscous and mix well. Stir in the black olives, basil, a drizzle of extra virgin olive oil and a squeeze of lemon, and season with a little more salt and pepper.

DOLCI
E BEVANDE

Sweets
& Drinks

Nonna absolutely loves anything lemon-flavoured, so I knew we had to make a lemon tart for this book. This one has got a soft buttery base and a rich, tangy and sweet filling that contains silken tofu, so it's actually got a bit of protein in it, too!

CROSTATA AL LIMONE
Sicilian Lemon Tart

SERVES: 8
PREP TIME: 1 hour 20 mins
COOKING TIME: 45 mins + chilling overnight

INGREDIENTS ◆

Pastry

100g vegan butter, straight from the fridge

200g plain flour, plus extra for dusting

50g caster sugar

a pinch of fine salt

2 tbsp cold water

Lemon filling

juice of 3–4 lemons (around 100ml)

zest of 1 lemon

150ml vegan double cream

30g cornflour

1 x 300g block of silken tofu, drained well

¾ tsp ground turmeric

190g caster sugar

40g vegan butter, melted

1. First make the pastry. Dice the butter roughly and put it into a food processor with the flour, sugar and salt. Pulse briefly until the mixture resembles fine breadcrumbs.

2. Add 2 tablespoons of cold water and pulse again until the mixture starts to come together in larger clumps. Tip this on to a lightly floured surface and very briefly knead it with your hands, just enough to bring it together into a smooth pastry. Don't worry if it feels very crumbly at first, just keep kneading until the warmth of your hands helps it to come together, and stop as soon as it's a smooth dough. If you knead it too long the pastry will become tough and will shrink in the oven.

3. Shape the pastry into a disc around 4cm thick. Wrap it in cling film and place it in the fridge for at least 1 hour.

4. Meanwhile, preheat the oven to 170°C fan/190°C and butter a 23cm loose-bottomed tart tin.

5. Once the pastry is ready, dust your work surface with flour and roll it out to just larger than your tin. Gently lift the pastry into the tin and press it into all the corners and up the sides. Trim off any excess. Put the lined tart back into the fridge for 10 minutes.

6. Before you add the filling, the tart case must first be baked blind. Take a sheet of baking paper larger than the tart and place it in the lined case. Fill it with baking beans or rice. Put the tart case into the preheated oven for 25 minutes, then remove the baking beans and paper. Return it to the oven for a further 10 minutes, or until the pastry looks cooked and is starting to turn golden.

7. Remove the tart case from the oven and place it on a wire rack to cool.

»

8. Meanwhile, to make the filling, combine all the ingredients in a blender and blitz until smooth (about 15–20 seconds).

9. Carefully pour the mix into the cooled tart case and bake for a further 30–35 minutes, until the filling has just set. It will feel very wobbly and loose at this stage but will firm up as it cools.

10. Remove the tart from the oven and leave to cool to room temperature. Refrigerate for a minimum of 4 hours or overnight (don't cut it too early, as it won't have set properly).

TIP ◆
Placing the tart tin on a hot tray in the oven helps the base cook evenly and quickly.

CHEF'S TIP ◆
It won't look as yellow before baking but gets much darker – don't worry, you won't taste the turmeric at all.

Sfinci – pronounced 'SFEEN-chee' – are a typical fluffy Sicilian doughnut made on St Joseph's Day. They're light and spongy (the name actually derives from spugna, meaning sponge), and are traditionally served with a sweet ricotta topping and candied fruit. When we made them for the photoshoot I think I ate about five that day, because they're that good.

SFINCI DI SAN GIUSEPPE
Fluffy Sicilian Doughnuts

MAKES: 6
PREP TIME: 4 hours
COOKING TIME: 1 hour

INGREDIENTS ◆

180ml soy milk

50g vegan butter

1 tsp vanilla paste or extract

250g self-raising flour

60g caster sugar

1 tsp baking powder

½ tsp fine salt

zest of 1 orange

1 litre vegetable oil, for deep-frying

Ricotta cream

75g cashews

75ml whippable vegan cream

1 tbsp caster sugar

½ tsp vanilla paste or extract

zest of 1 orange

To finish

6–12 long strips of candied orange peel, or 6 tsp candied mixed peel

50g chopped pistachios

6 glacé cherries

1. Before you start, soak the cashews in cold water for at least 4 hours or overnight.

2. Preheat the oven to 160°C fan/180°C.

3. Put the soy milk, butter and vanilla into a small saucepan and warm over a low heat until the butter has just melted. Remove and set aside to cool to tepid.

4. Meanwhile, put the flour, sugar, baking powder and salt into a large mixing bowl. Sprinkle over the orange zest and give it a good mix to incorporate everything.

5. Pour the vegetable oil into a medium saucepan (you want the oil to be at least 8–10cm deep, so don't use too wide a pan – roughly 18–20cm in diameter works well) and place over a medium heat. Line a tray or plate with kitchen paper.

6. While the oil is heating, make a well in the centre of your dry mix and pour in the milk and butter mix. Using a whisk or a wooden spoon, gradually start stirring to bring the mix together, just until all the flour is incorporated and you have a thick, smooth mix that is somewhere between a batter and a dough in consistency. If it looks like any lumps of flour haven't mixed in, give it a quick, vigorous stir and they should disappear.

7. When the oil has reached a temperature of 170°C, it's ready (if you don't have a thermometer, you can test by dropping a piece of bread into the oil – it should bubble and turn golden in about 20 seconds). With a large serving spoon, scoop up a portion of mix about the size of a large egg (a sixth of the dough, roughly).

Then use a second spoon to help you gently ease the mix off the first spoon and into the hot oil, being careful not to let the oil splash. Repeat with 2 more scoops of dough.

8. Fry for 5–6 minutes, until the doughnuts are golden brown. Use a metal slotted spoon to turn them over from time to time so they cook and colour evenly on all sides. Don't worry if they are slightly irregular in shape – they're not supposed to be perfectly circular. If they start to colour too quickly, turn the heat down. The oil needs to stay at a steady temperature. When the first 3 doughnuts are ready, remove them to the lined tray or plate using the slotted spoon. Repeat with the rest of the dough to make 3 more doughnuts.

9. Once all the sfinci are cooked, put them on a baking tray and transfer it to the oven for 5 minutes, to make sure they are fully cooked and crisp. Then place them on a wire rack and leave them to cool completely.

10. Meanwhile, make the ricotta cream. Drain the cashews, place them in a small blender with 30ml of the vegan cream, and blitz until smooth and creamy. If you don't have a small blender, pound the cashews in a pestle and mortar until smooth, then stir in the cream.

11. Pour the remaining cream into a large mixing bowl and add the sugar, vanilla and orange zest. Whisk until you have stiff peaks, then fold in the cashew mix.

12. Once the doughnuts are cool, top each one with a dollop of cream and garnish with orange peel, chopped pistachios and glacé cherries – if you like, you can cut a small 'v' shape into the top of the doughnut to place more cream on, and if you're serving a platter, you can slice a sliver off the bottom to prevent them toppling over!

miglie in
grinaggio a

an *Giuseppe*
padre putativo di Gesù Cristo
23

- AVVISO SACRO -

I promise you won't be able to tell that this panna cotta is dairy-free – it's smooth, decadent and has the perfect amount of wobble that a panna cotta should have! The secret ingredient . . . vege-gel! It's a plant-based alternative to gelatine that behaves exactly the same and doesn't leave a grainy or firm consistency like cornflour or agar agar would.

PANNA COTTA

Vanilla Panna Cotta with Caramel Sauce

MAKES: 4
PREP TIME: 15 mins
COOKING TIME: 2 hours

INGREDIENTS ◆

400ml plant-based double cream

100g caster sugar

3 tbsp coconut milk cream (the firm layer at the top of a tin of full-fat coconut milk)

1 tbsp vanilla paste

½ tbsp vege-gel

200ml soy milk

Caramel sauce
40g vegan butter

60g light brown sugar

1 tbsp black treacle

50g golden syrup

½ tsp vanilla paste

50g vegan double cream

2 tbsp coconut milk cream (see above)

TIP ◆

You can also eat these straight from a small glass cup if you don't have the moulds!

1. Lightly oil four pudding moulds or ramekins and set aside.

2. In a medium saucepan combine the double cream, caster sugar, coconut milk cream and vanilla paste.

3. Put the vege-gel into a measuring jug, then pour in the soy milk and whisk until the gel has dissolved. Add this to the pan of cream.

4. Place the pan over a medium-low heat and bring slowly to the boil, stirring regularly to prevent the cream catching.

5. As soon as it comes to the boil, remove the pan from the heat and pour the cream into the oiled moulds or ramekins. Leave to cool, then put into the fridge for at least 2 hours to fully set and chill.

6. Meanwhile, make the caramel sauce. Put the butter, sugar, treacle and golden syrup into a small pan and heat gently, stirring often, until the sugar and butter have melted and you have a smooth, glossy sauce. Bring to a simmer and let it bubble away for 2 minutes. Now add the vanilla paste, double cream and coconut milk cream. Mix well and let it simmer for 30 seconds more, then remove from the heat. At this stage it will look very thin, but it will thicken as it cools. Leave at room temperature until cooled.

7. To demould the panna cotta, gently dip the base of each mould into warm water for 30 seconds, then tip out on to a plate. If it doesn't come out first time, dip it in the water for a bit longer.

8. Drizzle the panna cotta with caramel sauce and serve the rest of the sauce in a jug on the side.

Hear me out! Vegan ladyfingers are impossible to find, and ain't nobody got time to make their own from scratch, so I thought why not use Biscoff biscuits? They're already coffee-flavoured, very accessible and accidentally vegan! This recipe uses whipped vegan double cream, but you can swap this out for 175g silken tofu to boost the protein!

TIRAMISU

SERVES: *6*
PREP TIME: *20 mins*
CHILLING TIME: *2 hours*

INGREDIENTS ◆

300ml freshly brewed espresso (or 300ml hot water mixed with 3 tbsp instant coffee if you're feeling lazy)

400g vegan cream cheese

100g caster sugar

1 tbsp vanilla extract

1 tbsp maraschino liqueur (optional)

400ml plant-based double cream, whipped

500g Biscoff biscuits

1 tbsp cocoa powder

1. Prep your coffee. It's best to use freshly brewed espresso coffee in a cafetière, but if you're in a rush, you can use instant. You'll need around 300ml.

2. In a separate bowl, add the cream cheese, sugar, vanilla and maraschino (if using) and whisk to combine. Then gently fold in the whipped cream using a spatula until all combined.

3. Dip each Biscoff biscuit in the coffee for no more than 1 second – just a quick dip in and out is enough, otherwise they will get too soggy. You may think it's not long enough, but trust me – in and out! Make two layers of biscuits in the bottom of a dish roughly 27 x 20cm, and cover them with half the cream cheese mixture. Make another two layers of the dipped biscuits, and finally add a second layer of cream cheese mixture.

4. Cover with cling film and refrigerate for 2 hours minimum, but ideally overnight. Dust with cocoa powder and crumble over some crushed Biscoff biscuits just before serving.

This is one of those cakes that you can give to someone and they'd never guess it's plant-based. Nonna and I like to make it with pears from her garden. It always tastes better the next day when all the pear juices have done their thing. The picture next to the cake is of Nonna and Nonno in Sicily on their 25th wedding anniversary, taken in 1983.

TORTA DI PERE
Pear Cake

SERVES: *8*
PREP TIME: *15 mins*
COOKING TIME: *1 hour*

INGREDIENTS ◆

7–8 firm pears (I use Conference pears, but Williams would also work well)

220g plant-based butter, softened, plus 2 tbsp melted butter for glazing

200g caster sugar

1 tsp vanilla extract

320g plain flour

3 tsp baking powder

3 tbsp demerara sugar

plant-based single cream/ice cream, to serve

1. Preheat the oven to 175°C fan/195°C. Grease and line a 25cm springform cake tin.

2. Peel two of the pears, then blend to form a purée.

3. In a mixing bowl, mix the butter and caster sugar together, using the back of a spoon to combine it into a smooth paste, then add your pear purée and vanilla extract. Use a whisk to mix well.

4. Sift in a quarter of the flour, while whisking. Switching to a large spoon or spatula, gently fold through the remaining flour and the baking powder.

5. Peel and cut two pears (approx. 300g) into roughly 1½cm cubes and fold them through the cake batter. Pour the mixture into the prepared tin and spread evenly.

6. Peel, halve and core the remaining 3 pears, then cut them into thin slices roughly 5mm thick. Arrange the slices on the top of the cake in a ring. Brush the pear slices with the melted plant-based butter and sprinkle over 2 tablespoons of demerara sugar.

7. Bake for 55–65 minutes, until golden and cooked through. You can check it's done by inserting a skewer into the middle of the cake. If the pears are browning too quickly, cover the cake loosely with a sheet of foil for the rest of the cooking time.

8. Once cooked, remove to a wire rack to cool before serving. Sprinkle with a final tablespoon of demerara sugar for an extra crunch, if you like. This cake goes great with plant-based cream or ice cream and fresh berries.

This dessert is simpler to make than you might think – it's a classic mix, filled with oozing melted dark chocolate and served with a creamy homemade coconut ice cream. I worked on this recipe with Giovann Attard, the head chef at one of my favourite Italian restaurants, Norma. I did my first-ever restaurant residency there for one night only, and sold out 150 slots in two hours!

TORTINO AL CIOCCOLATO
Salted Chocolate Tortino

MAKES: *3*
PREP TIME: *15 mins*
COOKING TIME: *15 mins*

INGREDIENTS ◆

Dry mix
110g plain flour or Tipo 00 flour
20g ground almonds
100g caster sugar
1½ tsp baking powder
a pinch of salt
¼ tsp ground cinnamon
2 tbsp cocoa powder

Wet mix
60g plant-based butter
115ml plant-based milk, at room temperature
2 tbsp aquafaba (liquid from tinned chickpeas)
½ tsp vanilla extract
¼ tsp moscatel vinegar or sherry vinegar

Filling
75g vegan dark chocolate (callets, or broken into chunks)

To serve
Coconut gelato (page 251)
Zia Lillina's Cobaita (page 266), or almond flakes, to garnish

1. Preheat the oven to 180°C fan/200°C. Place a tray of water on the bottom shelf of the oven (this will help keep the desserts moist while they cook).

2. Put the dry ingredients into a large bowl and mix with a fork to combine, then set aside.

3. For the wet mix, melt the butter in the microwave or on the hob, being careful not to let it burn. Pour the butter into a bowl or measuring jug, then gently stir in the room-temperature plant-based milk. While continuing to stir, add the aquafaba, vanilla and vinegar.

4. Make a well in the centre of the dry mixture, then gently pour in the wet mixture and whisk until combined.

5. Brush the pudding tins with softened butter in an upward motion, then sprinkle in some cocoa powder and roll the tin around, giving it a good shake, so the tin is fully coated on the inside with a layer of cocoa that sticks to the butter.

6. Fill each of the pudding tins one-third of the way up with the mixture, then add 25g of chocolate to the top of each one. Pour over the rest of the mixture to cover the chocolate, stopping at least 4cm from the top.

7. Place the tins on a baking tray and bake for 12–14 minutes.

8. Remove the chocolate puddings from their moulds, and serve on a plate with ice cream, cobaita or almond flakes and a dusting of icing sugar.

You'll find this dessert in most Italian bakeries – it's a soft shortcrust base filled with a super creamy custard filling that uses a ridiculously easy hack: Bird's custard powder, which just so happens to be accidentally vegan!

TORTA DELLA NONNA
Sicilian Custard Tart

SERVES: 6
PREP TIME: *1 hour*
COOKING TIME: *1 hour*

INGREDIENTS ◆

Custard
700ml oat or soy milk
100g caster sugar
zest of 1 lemon
½ tsp vanilla extract/ paste (or 1 vanilla pod)
35g Bird's custard powder (or any plant-based custard powder)
35g cornflour
70ml cold water

Pastry
350g plain flour
80g caster sugar
a pinch of fine salt
½ tsp baking powder
110g coconut oil, melted and cooled to just warm
80ml cold water

Decoration
40g pine nuts
icing sugar, for dusting

1. To make the custard, place the oat milk and sugar in a large saucepan, along with the lemon zest and vanilla. Bring the milk to a low heat, stirring occasionally. If using a vanilla pod, turn the heat off and leave to infuse for 10 minutes.

2. In a small bowl mix the custard powder with the cornflour, then add 70ml of cold water and stir until there are no lumps.

3. Pour this custardy liquid into the infused milk, whisking constantly, then bring to a medium heat. Continue to stir until the custard thickens up. Remove from the heat (discard the vanilla pod, if using). Immediately pour the custard into a large, heatproof bowl and lay a sheet of cling film or baking paper directly on top, to stop a skin forming. Set aside (but not in the fridge) for the custard to cool completely (this should take about 40 minutes).

4. To make the pastry, put the flour, sugar, salt and baking powder into a food processor (ideally one you can add liquid to while it's on). With it running on slow speed, gradually pour in the melted coconut oil until the mixture forms a breadcrumb texture.

5. Gradually pour in the cold water until the pastry just starts to come together into a clump.

6. Tip the pastry out on to a lightly floured work surface and bring it together into a smooth ball. Try not to work it too much as that will make the pastry tough.

7. Cut off one-third of the dough. This will be for the top of the tart. Using a rolling pin, gently shape this piece of dough and the remaining two-thirds into two discs roughly 1cm thick. Carefully wrap in cling film and put into the fridge to rest for 20–30 minutes, or until your custard has cooled.

»

8. Preheat the oven to 170°C fan/190°C and place a heavy baking tray in the oven to heat up. Grease a 20cm high-sided fluted tart tin with a little coconut oil.

9. To assemble your torta, take the larger disc of pastry (this will be the base), remove the cling film and place it on a lightly floured surface. If the pastry has been in the fridge for too long, you might need to leave it at room temperature to soften back up before rolling. Roll it into a wider circle about 4mm thick and slightly larger than your tart tin. Place it in the greased tart tin and gently press it into the sides of the tin, leaving any extra pastry overhanging. If the pastry cracks at all, just press it back together with your fingers – there needs to be zero cracks, so the custard doesn't leak!

10. Remove the cling film from the cooled custard. Give it a vigorous whisk to get it as smooth as possible (it may look a bit lumpy, but don't worry). Pour the cooled custard into the tin and smooth the top as level as you can. The custard should come about ½cm below the top of the tin, to leave room for the lid.

11. Roll out the smaller disc of pastry to a circle about 3mm thick. Brush the bits of overhanging pastry on the bottom layer with a little plant milk, to help the top layer stick, then gently place the lid on top of the tart. Carefully press the edges of the tart together to seal the lid, then trim any excess pastry off by pressing straight down with your fingertips on to the metal rim of the tart case (or use a small sharp knife).

12. Brush the top of the tart with a little plant milk and scatter over the pine nuts, pressing them down gently to help them stick.

13. Place the tart into the preheated oven, directly on the heavy baking tray, and bake for 40–45 minutes, until golden. Leave to cool completely, then place uncovered in the fridge or in a cool, dry place overnight. Dust with icing sugar before serving. It is vital that the tart cools and sets overnight, or the custard won't be firm enough to slice!

TIP ◆

If there are a few lumps in the custard, use a sieve when you pour it into the heatproof bowl.

Don't skip the cooling period for this dessert as it's very important to get a solid set.

Cannoli were the last dessert I ate before I decided to go plant-based! It was my cousin's birthday and the cake was a giant mountain of these sweet, ricotta-filled shells – they're such a classic Sicilian dessert, and Nonna absolutely loves them with pistachios, so I knew we had to work on a vegan recipe for this book.

CANNOLI

SERVES: *8–10*
PREP TIME: *1 hour*
COOKING TIME: *10 mins*

INGREDIENTS ◆

200g plain flour

1 tsp cocoa powder

20g caster sugar

30g softened vegan butter

1 tbsp Marsala wine or red wine vinegar

1 tsp vanilla paste or extract

85ml soy milk

1–2 litres vegetable oil, for frying

100g crushed pistachios

100g mixed peel (optional)

50g icing sugar, to serve

Ricotta cream

75g cashews

75ml whippable vegan cream

4 tbsp caster sugar

½ tsp vanilla paste or extract

EQUIPMENT ◆

Cannoli moulds, found online or in most kitchen shops

1. Before you start, soak the cashews in cold water for at least 4 hours or overnight.

2. Sieve the flour and cocoa powder into a large bowl. Add the sugar and mix with a fork until combined.

3. Cut the softened butter into small cubes. Mix it into the flour and sugar with your fingers until it's well combined.

4. Put the Marsala (or vinegar), vanilla and milk into a separate small bowl and mix vigorously to prevent the mixture from curdling.

5. Add the wet mix to the flour mix and combine first with a wooden spoon, then with your hands, until the dough comes together to form a firm brown ball. (You can use a stand mixer on a low setting for this.)

6. Knead the dough on a floured work surface for 5 minutes, until it becomes slightly softer, then shape it into a square about 6 x 6cm.

7. Wrap the square of dough in cling film and refrigerate for at least 3 hours or overnight.

8. Meanwhile, make the cashew ricotta. Drain the soaked cashews and put them into a small blender. Add 30ml of the vegan cream and blitz until smooth and creamy. If you don't have a small blender, pound the cashews in a pestle and mortar until smooth, then stir in the cream.

9. Pour the remaining cream into a large mixing bowl and add the sugar and vanilla. Whisk until you have stiff peaks, then fold in the cashew mix.

»

10. Remove the dough from the fridge. Cut it in half, then, using a floured rolling pin, roll each piece out on a floured surface into a very thin, long rectangle about 2mm thick. Use a pasta machine if you have one!

11. Put the oil into a deep saucepan or deep fryer and bring to 170–180°C. Line a plate with kitchen paper.

12. Cut out as many 10cm circles as you can from the dough, then carefully wrap one of the circles around your cannoli mould, intentionally leaving it quite loose at the edges. If it's too tight and doesn't reach, roll it out again to make it slightly thinner and bigger. Seal the dough around the cannoli mould with a dab of plant-based milk, then immediately transfer it carefully into the hot oil.

13. Let the cannoli fry for about 60 seconds, until it's nicely coloured and golden, and has also formed some bubbles. Place it on the paper-lined plate and let it cool, then carefully remove the cannoli mould and repeat. Be careful not to burn your fingers on the mould as it will be quite hot – using several at a time is a good idea!

14. Fill a piping bag with the ricotta mixture, or you can use a small spoon, then carefully fill each cannolo. Dip one end of the cannoli into the crushed pistachios and the other end in candied peel, if you like – have fun with it! Dust with icing sugar and enjoy!

I think Nonna's fruit salad was my first exposure to alcohol as a child, as she always likes to add a good glug of maraschino (her favourite cherry liqueur), which is absolutely optional but tastes bloody delicious! We'd have this most Sundays after dinner, alongside a regular dessert such as tiramisu or pear cake – and I think this is part of the reason why I love fruit so much as an adult, because Nonna made it taste so good when I was a child!

INSALATA DI FRUTTA
Nonna's Fruit Salad

SERVES: *2–3*

PREP TIME: *30 mins*

INGREDIENTS ◆

2 large apples (Nonna loves Pink Lady)

2 pears (Conference)

150g cherries

2 large oranges (Sicilian ones are the best, obviously)

2 peaches, depending on season

200g seedless grapes (red or green, or 100g of each)

Juice

450ml orange juice

1 tbsp sugar

juice of ½ a lemon

1 shot of maraschino (optional)

1. Wash all the fruit.

2. Put the orange juice into a large bowl. (You'll be adding the fruit straight into the bowl of juice.)

3. Peel and core the apples and pears, slice into 2½cm cubes, then add to the bowl.

4. Core the cherries and slice in half, then add to the bowl.

5. Peel the oranges and peaches, slice into wedges, remove any white pith from the oranges, and add to the bowl.

6. Slice the grapes in half and add them to the bowl.

7. Give everything a good mix, then add the sugar, lemon juice and maraschino.

8. Chill in the fridge for 30 minutes before serving.

Using olive oil in a cake sounds a bit strange, but I can assure you it works! In fact, I can't think of anything more Italian than using olive oil instead of butter in a cake. Make sure to use a good-quality extra virgin olive oil and you'll end up with a rich, moist and dense cake that tastes even better the next day.

TORTA ALL'OLIO CON PISTACCHIO
Pistachio & Olive Oil Cake

SERVES: 6
PREP TIME: *15 mins*
COOKING TIME: *30 mins*

INGREDIENTS ◆

150g ripe banana
  (approx. 2 bananas)
180g caster sugar
100ml olive oil
150g pistachios + 50g
  extra for presentation
150ml soy milk
1 tsp vanilla extract
zest of ½ a lemon
180g plain flour
50g finely ground
  polenta
½ tsp salt
1 tsp baking powder

Cherry compote
100g frozen cherries
50g caster sugar
juice of 1 lemon
3 tbsp water

I. Preheat the oven to 180°C fan/200°C.

2. Line a 24cm round springform cake tin with baking paper and grease the sides.

3. Peel the bananas and mash them in a small bowl with the back of a fork.

4. Add the sugar and combine with the banana.

5. Whisk together with an electric whisk, then slowly stream in the olive oil and continue whisking until combined. Set aside.

6. Toast 150g of the pistachios for 3–5 minutes on a medium heat in a dry non-stick pan, swirling the pan occasionally so they don't burn. They should go slightly darker in colour.

7. Blend the soy milk with the toasted pistachio nuts.

8. Add the blended soy milk to the bowl of banana, then stir in the vanilla extract and lemon zest and whisk again.

9. In a separate bowl, combine the dry ingredients (flour, polenta, salt, baking powder). Then sieve into the wet mix.

10. In a pestle and mortar, crumble down the remaining 50g of pistachios, then add to the cake mix and gently fold until all the dry mix is combined with the wet.

II. Pour into the cake tin and bake for 25–30 minutes, until a toothpick comes out dry.

12. Remove from the oven and cool on a wire rack.

13. Meanwhile, make the cherry compote. Put the cherries into a saucepan with the water and heat gently until they start to bubble, then add the sugar and lemon juice.

14. Stir well, using the back of a fork to mash the bigger pieces of fruit.

15. Let the compote cool, then pour over the slices of cake.

Zia Carmelina makes these every Christmas and New Year. Traditionally drizzled with honey and sugar strands, they are addictive! Pronounced kyah-kyeh-reh, they can also be made into small balls if you get bored of making the intricate swirls.

CHIACCHIERE
Carnival Biscuits

SERVES: *10*
PREP TIME: *35 mins*
COOKING TIME: *15 mins*

INGREDIENTS ◆

250g plain flour

50g caster sugar

15g baking powder

50g vegan butter, melted and cooled to just under room temperature (I use Flora)

1 tsp vanilla extract

1 small glass of white wine (125ml)

1 tbsp sunflower oil (or other neutral oil)

1–2 tbsp water

a pinch of fine salt

1 litre vegetable oil, for deep-frying

Decoration

Icing sugar

3–4 tbsp dark agave or any honey alternative

2 tbsp sugar strands (make sure you check these are vegan-friendly, as many are not!)

1. Put the flour, sugar and baking powder into the bowl of a stand mixer or food processor and mix for 30 seconds to combine.

2. With the mixer running on low, slowly add the melted vegan butter, vanilla extract, wine and sunflower oil. The mixture will start to come together to form a dough.

3. Gradually add the water until a stiff dough forms and let the machine knead the dough for 5 minutes.

4. Remove the dough from the bowl, wrap it in cling film and set aside at room temperature to rest for 30 minutes.

5. Lightly flour your work surface and divide the dough into 4 pieces. Take one of the pieces and, using a rolling pin, roll it into a square just under 1cm thick.

6. Using a pasta machine (or continuing with a rolling pin), roll the floured dough to roughly 1–2mm thickness.

7. Using a fluted pasta cutter or a knife, cut the dough into long strips the length of the dough. Cut these on the diagonal into 9 x 3cm strips, then cut a 2–3cm slit in the middle of each piece, leaving a border of 1cm on each edge. (Don't get rid of the offcuts; fry these too as they're just as delicious.) If you're unsure what these should look like, look at the photo on the next page.

8. This bit is a little tricky but worth it! You can fry them as they are, but Zia likes to fold the top point down through the slit and back up, and the bottom one up through the slit and down, to make a twist, basically the opposite way for each one.

»

Once cooled the chiacchiere freeze very well – Zia likes to keep batches frozen so there are always some ready for guests or to make a quick gift. Simply pop them into a ziplock bag without decorating and place them in the freezer with plenty of room so they don't break. When you're ready to eat them, just take them out, let them defrost for 20–30 minutes, then decorate.

9. Heat the vegetable oil in a large saucepan or deep fryer to 190°C (or until a piece of bread dropped into the oil sizzles and turns golden instantly), and prepare a large tray covered with kitchen paper.

10. Fry the chiacchiere in batches for 30–60 seconds, turning them over in the oil until they are golden on all sides. Remove with a slotted spoon on to the kitchen paper.

11. Keep frying them in batches until all the dough is used up.

12. Let them cool, and serve on a large platter either dusted liberally with icing sugar or drizzled with agave and topped with sugar strands.

I remember getting slices of this filled with Nutella from the local bakeries in Sicily as a child – and I wanted to make a plant-based hazelnut spread for this recipe. However, Nonna said it's better with apricot jam, so we settled for apricot jam.

CROSTATA DI ALBICOCCHE
Apricot Tart

SERVES: *8*
PREP TIME: *2 hours 30 mins*
COOKING TIME: *40 mins*

INGREDIENTS ◆

Pastry
240g plain flour
120g ground almonds
70g caster sugar
a pinch of fine salt
½ tsp baking powder
zest of 1 unwaxed lemon
190g vegan butter
  (I use Flora)
½ tsp vanilla extract
2½ tbsp cold water

Filling
350g good-quality
  apricot jam (or cherry
  works well too)
juice of ½ a small
  unwaxed lemon

Glaze
1 tbsp melted vegan
  butter
1 tsp plant-based milk
1 tsp maple or agave
  syrup

1. Put the flour, ground almonds, caster sugar, salt, baking powder and lemon zest into a large mixing bowl. Cut the vegan butter into small cubes and add to the bowl. Using the tips of your fingers, gently rub the butter into the dry ingredients until it resembles fine breadcrumbs (the same way as if you were making a crumble).

2. Add the vanilla extract and the water and mix until it just starts to form a dough. Tip the mix on to a lightly floured work surface and use your hands to bring it together until it has just formed a smooth dough. Don't overwork it or the pastry will be tough.

3. Cut a piece off the pastry weighing 250g (should be just under half the dough mix). This will be for the top of the crostata. Roughly mould it into a small, flat square about 2cm thick. Take the remaining dough and shape it into a 2cm-thick round. Wrap both blocks of pastry in cling film and refrigerate for at least 2 hours or overnight.

4. When you are ready to bake, preheat the oven to 170°C fan/190°C and place a large, heavy baking tray in the oven to heat up. Grease a 23cm round fluted tart tin with vegan butter.

5. Take the bigger block of pastry from the fridge, unwrap it and place it on a lightly floured surface. Roll it out to a circle 5–6mm thick and just slightly larger than your tart tin. Lift it into the tin and gently press it into the sides and base. Trim off any excess pastry from around the edge.

»

6. In a small bowl mix the jam and lemon juice until just combined. Spread this mix evenly over the base of the tart.

7. Place the tart back in the fridge while you roll the other block of pastry into a 23 x 23cm square. Cut this square into 14 strips, each around 1½cm wide.

8. Remove the tart from the fridge and carefully lay 7 strips vertically on top, spacing them out evenly. Repeat with the remaining 7 strips, laying them horizontally to form a lattice.

9. Around the edges, where the lattice pastry meets the pastry base, press together to attach the top to the bottom. Then trim off any overhanging excess pastry.

10. Place the tart back in the fridge to chill for 10 minutes while you prepare the glaze.

11. Mix the ingredients for the glaze in a small bowl. Carefully brush the glaze over the pastry, avoiding getting any in the jam if possible.

12. Place the tart case on the hot tray in the oven and bake for 35–40 minutes, until the top is golden and the jam is thick and bubbling.

13. Take out of the oven and leave to cool on a rack completely before removing from the tin and serving.

TIP ◆
Placing the tart tin on a hot tray in the oven helps the base cook evenly and quickly.

GELATO VEGANO

SERVES: *6–8*

Nothing says summer in Italy quite like stepping into a gelateria and walking around town with a brioche filled with your favourite flavour. There's a spot in Sicily near Nonna's called Cuspidi, where they do tonnes of vegan flavours and vegan brioche which Nonna and I love – so I knew we had to replicate our favourite flavours for this book. We have a decadent and rich cioccolato as well as a creamy almond and a soft coconut.

Coconut Gelato

INGREDIENTS ◆

2 x 400ml tins of
coconut milk

150g caster sugar

2 tsp cornflour

50ml liquid glucose

1. Put the coconut milk, sugar and cornflour into a medium sauce-pan, and squeeze in the liquid glucose. Cook over a medium-high heat and bring to the boil, stirring constantly. This should take about 5–10 minutes.

2. Once the mixture starts to bubble, remove from the heat and leave to cool to room temperature.

3. Once the mix has cooled, churn in an ice cream machine and freeze.

4. Remove from the freezer 5 minutes before serving.

TIPS ◆

Make sure the coconut milk you buy is the tinned one, and that it has a high percentage of coconut in the ingredients and doesn't have any emulsifiers.

Liquid glucose is really sticky, so squeeze it directly into the bowl!

Chocolate Gelato

INGREDIENTS ◆

150g caster sugar

50ml agave syrup

50g cocoa powder

600ml room-
temperature water

200g vegan 70% dark
chocolate, chopped
into small pieces

1. Put the caster sugar, agave syrup and cocoa powder into a large saucepan and pour in 200ml of water. Place over a medium heat and whisk well until it is smooth and lump-free, then bring to a simmer, whisking every so often, and let it bubble for 1 minute.

2. Remove from the heat and add the chocolate. Whisk until the chocolate has all melted, then pour in the remaining 400ml of water.

3. Using a stick blender or a jug blender, blitz the mix for 1 minute to make sure it is really well combined (this will help the texture of the gelato once it is frozen). Leave to cool completely.

4. Give the mix a final whisk (it will have thickened up considerably), then place in an ice cream machine and churn until it has a soft, scoopable texture. Freeze until ready to serve. If you don't have an ice cream machine, put the mix into a deep, freezer-safe container and place in the freezer. After 2 hours give it a stir to prevent any big lumps of ice crystals forming. Repeat after another 2 hours.

5. Once the gelato is fully frozen, remove it from the freezer and break it up into chunks. Place in a food processor and blend until smooth, then pour it back into the container and freeze for a further 2 hours, until frozen enough to serve.

Almond Gelato

INGREDIENTS ◆

150g flaked almonds

500ml almond milk

200ml agave syrup or golden syrup

½ tsp vanilla paste or extract

1 tsp almond extract

2 tbsp cornflour

350ml whippable vegan double cream (I use Elmlea)

3 tbsp caster sugar

1. Preheat the oven to 170°C fan/190°C. Spread the flaked almonds out on a baking tray and toast them, stirring once or twice, until they are a deep golden brown. This should take around 8–10 minutes.

2. Meanwhile, pour the almond milk into a medium saucepan and bring just to the boil over a medium heat. Add the agave syrup, vanilla paste and almond extract, and whisk well until the syrup has combined with the milk.

3. Put the cornflour into a small bowl and add 4 tablespoons of cold water. Stir well until you have a loose paste. Pour this into the hot almond milk, whisking continuously. Keep stirring while you bring the almond milk back up to the boil. It will thicken as it heats. Once it comes to the boil, let it bubble for 1 minute before removing from the heat.

4. Once the almonds are toasted, remove them from the oven and set aside 50g for later.

5. Add the rest of the hot almonds from the tray to the almond milk. Give it a stir, then set aside uncovered until totally cool. Once cool, cover the pan and place in the fridge overnight. This gives time for the almond milk to become infused with the flavour of the toasted almonds.

6. The next day, take the almond milk out of the fridge and pass it through a sieve into a bowl. Discard the almonds or set aside for use in something else.

7. Put the double cream and caster sugar into a large mixing bowl. Using an electric whisk, beat the cream until it forms stiff peaks. Gradually pour in the cold almond milk, while still whisking. Keep going until really well combined and whipped.

8. Pour into a freezable container and scatter over the 50g of reserved toasted almonds. Freeze overnight, then enjoy.

Granita is a typical Italian frozen dessert that's often served in coffee shops. There's a well-known granita bar called Bam Bar in Taormina that I visited when writing this book. It has tonnes of plant-based options, but my two favourite flavours are coffee and lemon, which Nonna always has a batch of somewhere at the back of her freezer.

GRANITA AL LIMONE
Lemon Granita

SERVES: 6
PREP TIME: 10 mins
FREEZING TIME: overnight

INGREDIENTS ◆

275g caster sugar

300ml water

200ml freshly squeezed lemon juice (roughly 7–9 lemons)

1. Put the sugar and water into a saucepan over a medium heat. Bring to the boil, then let it simmer for 1 minute. Remove from the heat and set aside to cool completely.

2. Meanwhile, squeeze your lemons and strain to remove any pips. I like to use one of those fancy lemon squeezers, which makes this part a lot easier.

3. Once the syrup is cool, stir in the lemon juice and pour the mix into a high-sided metal tray (such as a roasting tin or cake tin).

4. Put the tray into the freezer. After 1 hour, check the tray and give the mix a stir with a fork, gently breaking up any ice that is forming around the sides of the tin.

5. Return to the freezer and give it a mix with a fork every 30 minutes to break up the ice crystals, until the whole contents of the tray is made up of frozen clumps of ice crystals, like snow.

6. Transfer the granita to a freezer-safe container and put back into the freezer until you want to serve it.

7. Serve in small glasses or bowls.

GRANITA AL CAFFE
Coffee Granita

SERVES: *6*
PREP TIME: *10 mins*
FREEZING TIME: *overnight*

INGREDIENTS ◆

150g caster sugar
200ml water
400ml strong espresso

To serve (optional)
whipped plant-based
  cream
1 tbsp cocoa powder

1. Put the sugar and water into a saucepan over a medium heat. Bring to the boil, then let it simmer for 1 minute. Remove from the heat and pour in the coffee. Stir to combine thoroughly, then set aside to cool. Pour the mix into a high-sided metal tray (such as a roasting tin or cake tin).

2. Follow steps 4, 5 and 6 in the lemon granita recipe above to freeze and store your granita.

3. Serve in bowls, topped with a dollop of whipped cream and a dusting of cocoa powder if you like.

I know what you're thinking – a chocolate what? But this is actually a traditional Italian dessert, also known as salame Turcu (Turkish salami) in Sicily. Don't worry, there's no meat in this salami, just a mix of biscuits, nuts and dried fruit – it's kind of like a fancy rocky road.

SALAME DI CIOCCOLATO
Chocolate Salami

SERVES: *6–8*
PREP TIME: *10 mins*
CHILLING TIME: *2 hours*

INGREDIENTS ◆

200g 70% dark chocolate

50g vegan unsalted butter

1 tbsp coconut oil

1 tbsp agave or maple syrup

50g rich tea biscuits

40g soft dried figs

½ tsp vanilla extract

40g pistachios

30g pecans

Icing sugar

1. Break the chocolate into chunks and place them in a large, heatproof bowl with the butter, coconut oil and agave syrup. Place the bowl over a medium pan of barely simmering water (this is called a bain-marie) and leave to melt.

2. While the chocolate is melting, break the biscuits into a small bowl using your fingers. You want the pieces to be different sizes, no bigger than 2cm and no smaller than a chickpea size. Finely chop the figs.

3. Once the chocolate is all melted, take the bowl off the heat and add the vanilla, pistachios, pecans, biscuits and figs. Stir to combine everything. (You don't want to see any white bits!)

4. Place the mixture on a large piece of cling film and roll it into a sausage as tightly as you can, then tie the ends of the cling film together to keep it in place.

5. Place the chocolate salami in the fridge for 2 hours minimum.

6. Remove from the fridge and carefully remove the cling film (make sure none gets stuck). Dust the salami with icing sugar.

7. Slice into 1cm discs and serve.

8. You can store the chocolate salami in the fridge for weeks, or in the freezer for months!

These biscuits are unlike amaretti as they are soft and chewy with a subtle almond flavour that's sort of like marzipan. They pair well with a cup of tea and are great to make with kids as they're super simple.

PASTE DI MANDORLA

Sicilian Almond Biscuits

SERVES: *9*
PREP TIME: *15 mins*
COOKING TIME: *15 mins*

INGREDIENTS ◆

170g ground almonds

100g caster sugar

a pinch of fine salt

¼ tsp baking powder

½ tsp vanilla extract

60g aquafaba (liquid from a tin of chickpeas)

a pinch of cream of tartar (I use about ¼ tsp)

15–20 whole, unpeeled almonds

1. Preheat the oven to 170°C fan/190°C and line a large baking sheet.

2. In a large bowl combine the ground almonds, caster sugar, salt, baking powder and vanilla extract. Mix well.

3. Pour the aquafaba into a large, clean mixing bowl and add the cream of tartar. Using a handheld electric whisk, whisk for 5–6 minutes, until the aquafaba forms stiff peaks. Don't be tempted to stop whisking too early, as it needs the time to really hold its shape.

4. Very gently fold the whipped aquafaba through the almond mix using a metal spoon.

5. Wet your hands slightly, then take a heaped teaspoon (roughly 15g) of dough and roll it into a ball. Place on the baking sheet, then repeat with the remaining dough, spacing the balls out evenly and leaving at least 4cm between them.

6. Take the almonds and press one into the top of each of the biscuits. This will flatten the balls ever so slightly.

7. Bake in the preheated oven for 12–15 minutes, or until the biscuits are beautifully golden.

8. Remove from the oven and leave to rest for 10 minutes, then transfer to a wire rack to cool completely.

A tasty, sweet snack with a subtle pistachio flavour – I love them fresh out of the oven but also once they cool, they have a great crunch.

PASTE DI PISTACCHIO
Pistachio Biscuits

MAKES: *10*
PREP TIME: *1 hour*
COOKING TIME: *15 mins*

INGREDIENTS ◆

1 tbsp ground golden flaxseed (bought whole and ground in a small spice grinder)

3 tbsp cold water

100g pistachios

75g ground almonds

a pinch of salt

75g icing sugar, plus 30g for dusting

1 tsp maple syrup (also works well with 1 tsp agave syrup)

1. In a small bowl stir together the ground flaxseed and cold water and set aside for 10 minutes to thicken.

2. Place the pistachios in a small grinder and pulse until just finely ground. Be careful not to grind them too much or they will turn to nut butter.

3. In a large mixing bowl combine the ground pistachios, ground almonds and salt, then sift in 75g of icing sugar. Stir to combine.

4. Pour in the flaxseed mix and the maple syrup and, using a wooden spoon, stir to combine into a dough. The mixture will feel dry to begin with but a good mix will bring it together.

5. Cover the bowl with cling film and refrigerate for 1 hour.

6. Preheat the oven to 170°C fan/190°C, and grease and line a large baking tray.

7. Divide the dough into 10 balls, each roughly the size of a golf ball. Roll each ball into a sausage shape 9cm long, then form it into an 'S' shape and press down gently to flatten slightly.

8. Sift the remaining 30g of icing sugar into a shallow bowl and roll each biscuit in icing sugar to coat. Give a gentle shake to remove any excess and place on the prepared baking tray, spacing them evenly on the tray.

9. Bake for 10–15 minutes, until lightly golden. Remove from the oven and leave to stand for 5 minutes, then carefully transfer to a metal rack to cool completely (they will feel soft at this stage but will firm up as they cool).

PISTACHIO BISCUITS

AMARETTI THINS

SICILIAN ALMOND BISCUITS

Amaretti biscuits have a unique and rich almond taste, and are traditionally super light and airy. After trying a few ways to make these plant-based, we saw that they weren't rising the same as the traditional version, but they became incredibly crunchy and tasted exactly the same – so give these a go and thank me later!

BOCCONCINI DI MANDORLA
Amaretti Thins

MAKES: *18–24*
PREP TIME: *25 mins*
COOKING TIME: *20 mins*

INGREDIENTS ◆

150g whole skin-on almonds

75g icing sugar

½ tsp salt

1 tsp baking powder

100g aquafaba (liquid from tinned chickpeas)

¼ tsp cream of tartar

100g caster sugar

1 tbsp cornflour

1 tsp almond extract

75g plain flour

1. Preheat the oven to 170°C fan/190°C. Spread the almonds on a baking tray and place in the oven for 10–12 minutes, until nicely roasted. To check if they are ready, cut one in half – the inside should have a slight golden colour (instead of a creamy white). Once roasted, transfer the almonds to a plate to cool completely. Leave the oven on.

2. Once the almonds have fully cooled, put them into a food processor. Add the icing sugar and pulse until the almonds and sugar are fully combined and have become a fine, golden brown powder (this may take 2–3 minutes, scraping the sides in between pulses if needed). Transfer to a large mixing bowl. Add the salt and baking powder and stir well to combine.

   Put the aquafaba and cream of tartar into a separate, very clean mixing bowl (or the bowl of a stand mixer). Mix with an electric hand whisk (or in the stand mixer) on medium speed for 5 minutes, until the aquafaba is very thick and is standing in stiff peaks. Now start gradually adding the caster sugar a tablespoon at a time, while continuing to whisk. You should whisk for a further 5–6 minutes, until all the sugar is incorporated and you have a glossy meringue. Don't be tempted to whisk for less time – it really needs to be well whisked. Finally, shower in the cornflour and whisk for 30 seconds to combine.

3. Using a spatula or a metal spoon, take a third of the meringue and add it to the bowl of blitzed almonds and sugar along with the almond extract. Fold the meringue into the dry mix. For this stage you can be relatively vigorous, as you want it all to be incorporated to make a paste-like mix. Now add the rest of the

meringue and fold it in very gently – you want to retain as many air bubbles as possible. Once it is all folded in evenly, gradually shower in the plain flour using a sieve, while folding it through the mix.

4. Spoon the mix into a piping bag fitted with a round nozzle and pipe little mounds the size of a 1p coin on to a lined baking sheet, making sure to leave at least 2cm between them to allow them to spread. If you don't have a piping bag, just use a teaspoon!

5. Bake for 16–18 minutes, or until the biscuits are a deep golden colour and cracked on top. Remove them from the oven and leave to rest for 10 minutes, then transfer them to a rack to cool completely.

Nonna
APPROVED

You'll need to have strong teeth for this! Cobaita, also known as torrone, is a sweet and crunchy dessert made from only two ingredients – almonds and sugar. There's never a time when there's not a block of this somewhere in Nonna's house. When it runs out she makes more, and every time she brings it out, there's always a divide between those who absolutely love it and those who can't hack it! For me, as soon as I have one piece, I can't stop. Plus, it's 50% almonds, so it's healthy, right?

COBAITA
Crunchy Almond Brittle

SERVES: *6–8*
PREP TIME: *5 mins*
COOKING TIME: *10 mins*

INGREDIENTS ◆

350g caster sugar
350g raw, skin-on
  almonds
chocolate chips
  (optional)

TIPS ◆

The recipe ratio is exactly 1:1, so you can easily adjust it to whatever quantity you wish to make.

To quickly spread out the cobaita, grease a second sheet of baking paper and place over the top as soon as you pour the mix on to the first sheet. Gently use a rolling pin over the paper to spread the almonds out and get an even finish.

1. Lightly grease a large sheet of baking paper and set it aside on a heatproof surface (such as a large chopping board or baking tray).

2. Put the sugar into a large saucepan and shake to evenly cover the base of the pan. Place the pan over a medium heat until the sugar melts. Swirl the pan every so often but do not stir. Leave it over the heat until the sugar has just turned to a rich amber liquid. Be careful not to let it get dark and start to smoke, as this will mean it's burnt.

3. Lower the heat, add the almonds and stir until evenly coated, then turn the heat off.

4. Carefully pour the mixture on to the baking paper and, working quickly before it starts to set, use a wooden spoon to spread it to a thin layer around 1–2 almonds in height. Optionally, at this point you can sprinkle over some chocolate chips, which is what Nonna's sisters love to do in Sicily.

5. Allow to cool to room temperature, then break it apart and it's ready to eat.

6. Store in a container in the fridge or in a cool, dry place.

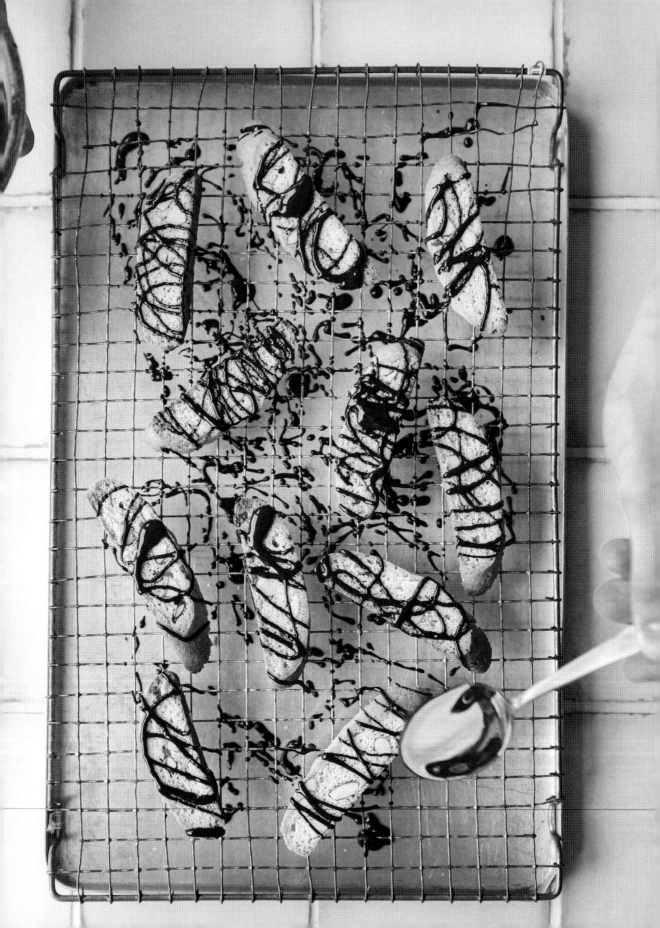

Biscotti literally translates to twice cooked (Bis-cotti). Nonna would always make these on special occasions and I remember always dipping them in her cup of tea until they went soft because they were too crunchy for my teeth. They make a great gift!

BISCOTTI
Crunchy Almond Biscuits

MAKES: *24 biscuits*
PREP TIME: *15 mins*
COOKING TIME: *30 mins + another 10 mins*

INGREDIENTS ◆

70ml plant-based milk
70ml vegetable oil
1 tsp vanilla extract
25g icing sugar
100g caster sugar
75g skin-on almonds
240g plain flour
1 tsp baking powder

TIPS ◆

Flip your biscotti during the second bake, as this will allow them to bake evenly on both sides for that beautiful, bakery-style finish.

If you have a sweet tooth, dip the finished biscuits in 100g melted dark chocolate and set aside to cool.

1. Preheat the oven to 180°C fan/200°C and line a large baking tray with baking paper.

2. Mix the plant-based milk, oil and vanilla together.

3. Sift both sugars into a large mixing bowl, then add your plant-based milk mixture and whisk until combined.

4. Put the almonds into a food processor and give them a quick blitz, not too finely as you want to keep their crunch. Alternatively you can roughly chop them by hand. Stir them into the biscuit mixture.

5. While whisking, gradually shower in the flour and baking powder and mix until a soft dough starts to form.

6. Transfer the dough to a floured work surface and divide it into 2 equal portions. Take one portion of dough and gently roll it into a log shape roughly 4cm in diameter and 26–28cm long. Repeat with the second portion of dough.

7. Lift the logs on to the lined baking tray, leaving at least 5cm between them. Place the baking tray in the oven and bake for 25–30 minutes, or until lightly browned, then remove from the oven and leave to cool for 10–15 minutes.

8. Cut the logs into diagonal slices roughly 1½cm thick and place them back on the baking tray, cut side up.

9. Return the tray of biscotti to the oven for a second bake of 10 minutes, for that extra crunch.

10. Enjoy your crunchy, flavourful biscotti with your favourite cup of tea or coffee.

Limoncello, not LEMON-cello, is a southern Italian liquor made from – you guessed it – lemons. Nonno would often leave guests with a cold shot of limoncello after dining in the restaurant, so this recipe is dedicated to him. When I recently took a few friends to Nonna and Nonno's for dinner, it came as no surprise to me when Nonno walked in with a big bottle for us all to take shots from.

LIMONCELLO

MAKES: *1 litre*
PREP TIME: *3 weeks*

INGREDIENTS ◆

5 large unwaxed lemons
500ml vodka
250g caster sugar

1. Peel the lemons, making sure not to press too hard – you don't want to remove too much of the white pith with the peelings. If your peelings do have a lot of white pith on them, place them flat on a chopping board and run a small knife over them to remove the pith from the lemon skin. It will make the limoncello bitter if you leave it on.

2. Place the vodka and lemon peelings in a large Kilner jar or any airtight glass container. Close the jar and leave for 7 days, shaking the jar once a day. The vodka will turn a vibrant yellow.

3. After 7 days, put the caster sugar into a small saucepan with 250ml water and place over a medium heat. Bring to the boil, then reduce the heat and simmer for 1 minute. Remove from the heat and leave to cool. Pour the sugar syrup into the jar of lemon vodka and stir well to combine.

4. Leave for a further week, then strain out the lemon peelings.

5. Serve chilled, in small glasses.

Nonna and I celebrated my cousin's wedding in Ravello, on the Amalfi Coast, a few years back – the whole town was filled with lemon everything, and this was where I first tried a limoncello spritz. You may have heard of an Aperol spritz, but this limoncello spritz is bursting with flavour and the rosemary and lemon go great together. You can buy your limoncello, but if you're feeling extra fancy, on page 270 I have a recipe for making your own at home.

LIMONCELLO SPRITZ

SERVES: 4
PREP TIME: 5 mins

INGREDIENTS ◆

125ml limoncello

25ml freshly squeezed lemon juice

75ml simple sugar syrup

ice cubes

300ml prosecco

soda water, to top up (about 100ml)

4 lemon slices

4 sprigs of rosemary (optional)

1. Combine the limoncello, lemon juice and sugar syrup in a jug and stir well to combine.

2. Fill 4 wine glasses with ice cubes and divide the limoncello mix evenly between them.

3. Pour some prosecco into each glass.

4. Finally add a splash of soda water and give each glass a quick stir.

5. Top each spritz with a slice of lemon and a sprig of rosemary, if you like.

TIP ◆

To make a simple sugar syrup, combine 100g of caster sugar and 100ml of water in a small saucepan. Stir well and place over a medium heat. Bring slowly to a simmer and allow to boil for 30 seconds, then remove from the heat and leave to cool completely. The syrup will keep in an airtight jar in the fridge for a month. Alternatively, you can buy sugar syrup from most supermarkets.

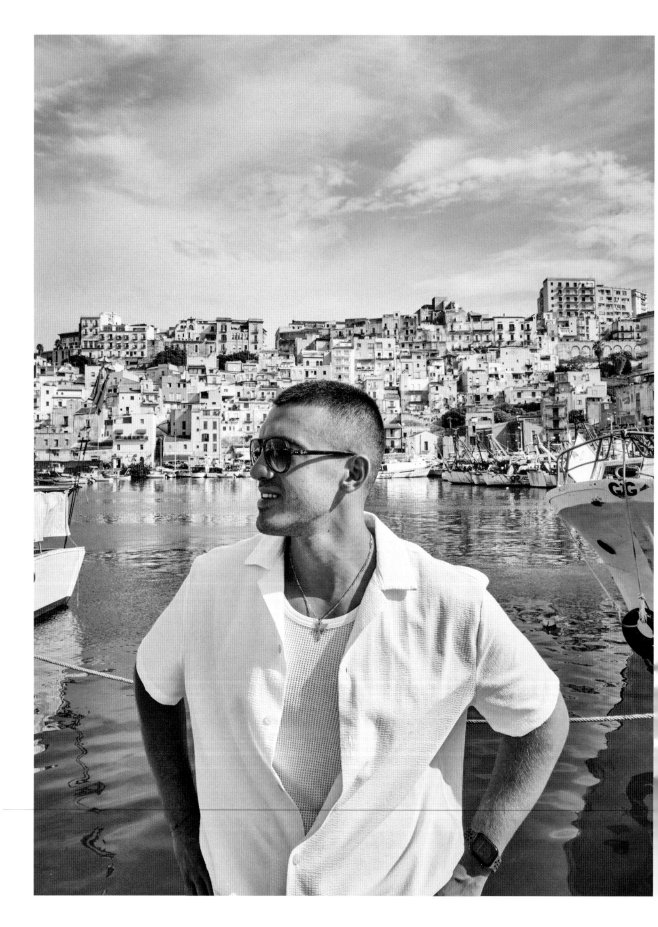

Not to be confused with a black coffee, this historical Italian cocktail was the first cocktail ordered by James Bond in *Casino Royale*. Traditionally served with a wedge of lemon or orange, this version makes the most of one of my favourite fruits, the Sicilian blood orange.

Traditionally it is made with Campari, which is technically not vegan-friendly due to the clarification process, but there are some great vegan alternatives like Contratto Bitter or Luxardo Bitter Rosso.

Make sure the vermouth you buy is vegan-friendly (e.g. Contratto Vermouth Rosso).

BLOOD ORANGE AMERICANO

SERVES: *2*
PREP TIME: *5 mins*

INGREDIENTS ◆

80ml red vermouth (vegan)

80ml Contratto Bitter or Luxardo Bitter Rosso

100ml soda water

2 slices of blood orange plus a squeeze of juice

1. Fill two lowball glasses with ice and divide the vermouth and Contratto Bitter between the glasses, then add a squeeze of blood orange juice to each. Stir well to combine.

2. Add a splash of soda to each, give it a light stir, and finish with a slice of blood orange to garnish.

A gimlet is a classic cocktail usually made with just gin, lime juice and sugar syrup, but this one has a Sicilian twist using grapefruit and mint.

SICILIAN-STYLE GRAPEFRUIT MINT GIMLET

SERVES: *2*
PREP TIME: *5 mins*

INGREDIENTS ◆

50ml sugar syrup
20 fresh mint leaves
80ml gin
100ml fresh grapefruit juice (approx. 1 large grapefruit)
1 tsp cherry essence/ syrup (optional)
extra grapefruit and mint, for garnish

1. If preparing your own sugar syrup, see page 273.

2. Remove the mint leaves from the stems and put them into a cocktail shaker with the sugar syrup. Give them a bit of a muddle by mashing them with a spoon or muddler to release the flavours.

3. Add the gin, grapefruit juice and cherry essence (if using) to the shaker. Add more syrup to reach your preferred level of sweetness.

4. Top the shaker with ice, then close the lid nice and tight and give it a good shake for 30 seconds.

5. Pour the cocktail into chilled glasses, and garnish with a grapefruit slice and a fresh sprig of mint.

Traditionally served with whipped egg white, this vegan version uses whipped chickpea water, aka aquafaba.

AMARETTO SOUR

SERVES: *4*
PREP TIME: *5 mins*

INGREDIENTS ◆

100ml aquafaba (liquid from tinned chickpeas)
1 tbsp caster sugar
300ml Disaronno
1 tbsp agave syrup
juice of 1 large lemon
1 tbsp cherry liqueur
4 candied cherries

1. Measure the liquid from the tin of chickpeas into a large bowl. Add the caster sugar, then, using an electric whisk, whip it until it just starts to have a frothy mousse texture that's still quite thick. If you overdo it, it will become stiff peaks, which we don't want!

2. Put the Disaronno, agave syrup, lemon juice and cherry liqueur into a small blender or cocktail shaker (add ice if using a cocktail shaker). Mix for 30 seconds, then strain into ice-filled glasses.

3. Evenly divide the whipped chickpea liquid between the glasses.

4. Top with a candied cherry on a toothpick and enjoy.

INDEX

THANKS

Working on this cookbook has been one of the most difficult yet rewarding projects of my life. There have been times where I've doubted if I'm even qualified enough to write it, and even now that it's finished, I still have massive imposter syndrome, but even though it's my name on the cover, there are a lot, and I mean **a lot** of people that made this book possible – including **you!**

Life often has defining moments that you don't realise until later just how important they are. For me, one of those moments was the night I won the Fortnum & Mason Creator of the Year award 2023. I took Nonna on stage and it was a moment I'll cherish forever, so I owe a huge thanks to the team at Fortnum's for that and also everyone who voted for me to win. On that night I was introduced to a man that would change my life – Daniel Hurst. Dan is my publisher at Penguin Michael Joseph and is the reason this book exists. Thank you, Dan! That night I also got chatting to Scott Anderson, a producer at *Saturday Kitchen*. A couple weeks later, Nonna and I were cooking live on BBC 1 for our first ever TV appearance. Thank you, Scott, and the whole *Saturday Kitchen* team.

To Sarah, Aggie, Hattie, Gaby, Ciara, Bea, Annie, Louise, and everyone else at PMJ – thank you for believing in this book and for being the most welcoming team. You made this experience such a dream and are all so incredibly talented. Extra special thanks to Louise for squeezing out extra budget when I insisted a trip to Sicily was necessary.

Next up, Lord (otherwise known as David) Loftus. I first came across David when he shot my friend Sam Way's cookbook and thought he looked pretty cool. Little did I know he is one of the most well-regarded photographers of our time and has shot Nigella Lawson, Gordon Ramsey, and pretty much every single Jamie Oliver book – so I couldn't quite believe (and still can't) that he agreed to shoot this random bloke and his nan and travel all the way to Sicily to do it! David, you're one of the most down to earth and humble people I know and I'm genuinely so grateful that you agreed to shoot this book.

Thanks to Rachel Mills for being the best book agent I could ask for and for teaching me all about how the industry works. My managers Emily and Andrea at The VTA for being the best managers and friends throughout this process, always being there for any support, and keeping me busy with brand partnerships.

Thanks to Robbie and Klaus for giving me my first proper job in the plant-based scene and giving me a reason to move to London. Henry and Ian at Bosh! for giving me work in the food scene and letting me quit to then do social media full time only a few months later.

To Hanna Miller, thank you for helping me turn Nonna's dishes into recipes that people can actually follow and understand, arguably one of the hardest tasks! And thank you also for being a fantastic recipe tester and food stylist. And to Hanna's assistants Eden, Isabel and Georgia – you guys were all such a pleasure to work with.

Thanks to Giovann too, who headed up my first ever restaurant residency at Norma, Charlotte St, and also helped with a couple special recipes in this book.

Now for the most important people to thank, my family. First, my Mum. There's no way any of this would be possible without you, you're always behind the scenes when I'm filming with Nonna cleaning up, making sure Nonna understands what I've said often translating when she doesn't, and you've always put others before yourself. You even washed the dishes on the shoot for this book.

To Dad, thanks for being the first person to teach me how to run a business, to treat all people with kindness and respect, and for always supporting me in anything I do. You've never pressured me to get a real job even when it meant taking photos of our family dinners and eating them cold, so thank you.

To my sister, Elisia. You are a constant rock of support in my life, always suggesting recipes for me, giving me honest feedback and showing me just how to become a better person and creator. Thank you.

To Nonna's sisters and all the family in Italy. Zia Felicina, Zia Lillina, Zia Isabella, Zia Giuseppina, and Nonna Norina (their Mother) who gave birth to all of them! You made this book so special by being involved in the shoot, cooking all of your dishes for us all to eat together, and welcoming the whole team to your homes despite having no idea what it was really all for. Also a special thanks to Nonna's first child, my Zia Carmelina, for letting us shoot some of the book at your lovely house, it made Nonna feel so comfortable and I'll cherish those days forever.

To Nonna. Thank you for being the best Nonna I could ask for, you came to this country so young yet still managed to build several businesses and raise six kids.

There are no words to describe how blessed I am to be on this journey with you, I'll never be able to repay you for everything you've done for me both growing up and in my career, but this book is a small step in that direction. Thank you, Nonna for always being up for everything I ask, and always doing it graciously with a big smile on your face. You are the perfect example of what it means to be a loving, caring and selfless Nonna and I'm so grateful for every day I get to spend with you. One of my favourite quotes that sums this up for me is from the late Jamal Edwards, 'the goal isn't to live forever, it's to create something that will'.

Nonno. Thank you for letting me whisk Nonna away to Sicily, and regularly to London, and for the occasional cameo in my videos. But most of all for teaching me to always treat people with kindness and respect, and also the occasional card trick.

Now, to my friends, I am so grateful to be surrounded by so many. You know who you are, but a special thanks to my good friends Liam, Calum, Elly, Nic, Matt, Nguyen, Zena, and all the plant boiis and wiggedy fam, your support and friendship means everything to me. And a special shoutout to my Instagram Mum Juliet Sear.

Thanks also to all of my friends on social media who always like, comment and support my content. It genuinely means so much to me and I'm so grateful to those who have stuck around throughout my career and also to the new ones! Special thanks to all of Nonna's superfans who comment on every single video (looking at you, Steph Elswood!).

To Bel, aka the future prime minister - thank you for all the opportunities you have given to me throughout my career, I'm so grateful for you.

Thank you to the legends that kindly endorsed this book, Gennaro, Rachel, Liam, and Rav.

Finally, to you reading this right now, thank you from the bottom of my heart. This book isn't just about food – it's a celebration of the incredible people who've touched my life along the way.

Sepps x

michael joseph

UK | USA | Canada | Ireland | Australia
India | New Zealand | South Africa

Michael Joseph is part of the Penguin
Random House group of companies
whose addresses can be found at
global.penguinrandomhouse.com.

First published in Great Britain by
Michael Joseph, 2024
001

Set in Futura, CCDutchCourageDark,
TT Backwards Script and Mostra Nuova

Colour reproduction by Altaimage Ltd
Printed in Germany by Mohn Media GmbH

A CIP catalogue record for this book is
available from the British Library

ISBN: 978–0–2416–7798–8

www.greenpenguin.co.uk

Penguin Random House is committed to a
sustainable future for our business, our readers
and our planet. This book is made from Forest
Stewardship Council® certified paper.

Buon appetito!